CONTENTS

D0624285

PRICE/STERN/SLOAN
Publishers, Inc., Los Angeles
1981

CLEANING AGENTS

Throughout this book reference is made to the general cleaning agents and terms listed here. Given below are specific brand names for each general cleaner. Others are available through supermarkets, drugstores, and hardware stores. Cleaning agents are often poisonous, so keep well away from children. Only use bottles provided and label them carefully. They are often inflammable and sometimes give off toxic fumes.

- *Never smoke while using.*
- *Never use near an open fire.*
- *Always have proper ventilation (open windows, etc.).*

ABRASIVE CLEANERS: *Ajax, Comet, Bon Ami* (powders); *Soft Scrub* (liquid). From supermarkets.

ABRASIVE PAPER: Glasspaper, sandpaper, emery paper, wet and dry paper. From hardware stores.

ABSORBENT PADS: Cottonwool, *Kleenex*, paper napkins, soft white cloth.

ABSORBENT POWDERS: Fuller's earth, kitty litter, sawdust (for hard surfaces), French chalk, powdered starch, talcum powder (for fabrics). All absorbent powders listed above are harmless to surfaces but may be difficult to remove from dark, non-washable fabrics.

ACIDIC ACID: See White Vinegar.

ACETONE: From drugstores. Fabrics: Harmless to most natural and synthetic fibers. Inflammable. Toxic fumes. See also Amyl Acetate.

- *Never use on acetate, triacetate, modacrylic and rayon.*
- *Always test first.*

ALCOHOL: From drugstores. Inflammable.

- *Always dilute for use on acetate.*
- *Always test first.*

ALL-PURPOSE CLEANERS: *Fantastik, Formula 409* (spray); *Mr. Clean, Ajax, Lysol, Top Job.* From supermarkets.

- *Always follow instructions.*

AMMONIA (HOUSEHOLD): From supermarkets, hardware stores. Use white vinegar or lemon juice solution if ammonia affects color. Use solution of 1 tablespoon to 1 pint water. Sponge or soak for about 3 minutes. If spilled on skin, wash immediately then apply vinegar or lemon juice. Poisonous. Toxic fumes.

- *Never use on silk, wool or their blends.*
- *Never use undiluted.*
- *Never let it dry on the fabric.*
- *Always follow instructions.*
- *Always rinse well after use.*
- *Always test first.*

AMYL ACETATE: From drugstores. Fabrics: Use instead of acetone on acetate, triacetate, modacrylic and rayon. Non-oily nail polish remover is a substitute. Inflammable. Toxic fumes.

- *Never use on plastics.*
- *Always test first.*

ANTISEPTIC: *Lysol, Listerine, Pine-Sol.* From supermarkets.

ART GUM ERASER: From artist's supply stores.

BATH/BATHROOM CLEANERS: *Dew, Lysol Basin/Tub/Tile Cleaner, Bathroom Fantastik, Lysol* (sprays). From supermarkets.

- *Always follow instructions.*

BICARBONATE OF SODA: From drugstores, hardware stores and supermarkets.

BLEACH: See Chlorine Bleach, Hydrogen Peroxide and Wood Bleach.

BORAX: From supermarkets. Harmless to most fabrics. Use 1 tablespoon borax to 1 pint water. Soak for about 10 minutes. Can be used directly on white fabrics.

- *Always test first.*

CARPET SHAMPOO/SPOT REMOVERS: *Carbona, Spray N' Vac, Lestoil Rug Shampoo, Glory Rug Cleaner, Plush Dry Cleaner, Woolite.* From supermarkets and hardware stores.

- *Always follow instructions.*

CEMENT & CONCRETE CLEANER: Muriatic Acid. From hardware stores.

CHLORINE BLEACH: *Clorox, Purex.* From supermarkets. Use 1 tablespoon liquid bleach to 1 pint cold water. Sponge or soak for 5-15 minutes. Repeat if needed. Poisonous.

- *Never mix with other cleaning agents.*
- *Never use on silk, wool, mohair, leather, linen, rayon, elastane, drip-dry or dark-colored cottons, flame-proof or crease-resistant finishes.*
- *Never use undiluted.*
- *Never store in a metal container.*
- *Never use on or with metal objects.*
- *Always follow instructions.*
- *Always rinse well afterwards.*
- *Always test first.*

CHROME CLEANER: *Brasso, Noxon.* From hardware stores.

- *Always follow instructions.*

CREAM OF TARTAR: From supermarkets.

DENTURE CLEANER: *Efferdent, Polident, Mersene.* From drugstores.

DETERGENT POWDERS: *Ajax, Tide, Cheer, Dash, Cold Power XL, Bold 3, Fab.* Best used on hot setting. Use lather only on non-washable fabrics.

DETERGENT POWDERS (MILD): *Ivory Snow, Arm and Hammer.* From supermarkets. Milder than detergent powders. Fabrics: May be used directly on some stains.

DETERGENT POWDERS (ENZYME): *Oxydol, Axion.* From supermarkets.

- *Never use on wool, silk, non-colorfast, flame-resistant or rubberized fabrics.*
- *Never soak zippers or other metal fastenings.*
- *Always test first.*
- *Always follow instructions.*

DETERGENTS, LIQUID: See Dishwashing Liquid Solution.

DEVELOPER: From photographic stores. Use ½ teaspoon to ½ pint warm water.

DISTILLED WATER: From drugstores and supermarkets.

DRAIN CLEANER: *Liquid Plumber, Drano.* From supermarkets.

- *Always follow instructions.*

DRY-CLEANER SOLUTION: *K2R Spot Remover, Goddard's Dry-Cleaner.* From supermarkets and hardware stores. Apply only to dry surfaces. Treat several times with a mild solution instead of once with a strong solution. Inflammable. Toxic fumes.

- *Never use on leather, suede, rubber, plastics or waterproofed fabrics.*
- *Never use in a washing machine.*
- *Always follow instructions.*

EUCALYPTUS OIL: From drugstores. Use undiluted. May smell during and after use.

FLOOR POLISH: *Klear, Future, Mop & Glow, Step Saver, Shine Guard, Jubilee, Finis, Perk.* From supermarkets and hardware stores.

- *Always follow instructions.*

FURNITURE POLISH: *Favor, Old English, Pledge, Behold, Scott's Liquid Gold, Complete.* From supermarkets and hardware stores.

- *Always follow instructions.*

GLASS/WINDOW CLEANERS: *Ajax Window Cleaner, Glass Plus, Windex.* From supermarkets and hardware stores.

- *Always follow instructions.*

GLYCERINE: From drugstores. Safe to use on most fabrics. Use diluted in equal parts with warm water. Rub into fabric and leave for up to an hour to soften stain. Rinse well with warm water after use.

GLYCERINE SOAP: *Esquire Soap, Pears Soap,* any equivalent of saddle soap. From drugstores.

- *Always follow instructions.*

HYDROGEN PEROXIDE: From drugstores. Buy 20 volume strength. See text for instructions. Fabrics: Use 1 part 20 volume strength peroxide to 4 parts cold water and add a few drops of ammonia.

- *Never use on nylon or flame-resistant fabrics.*
- *Never add ammonia if the fabric is silk, wool or colored.*
- *Always test first.*

IODINE: From drugstores.

IRON (PRESSING) CLEANER: *Vilene.* From hardware stores.

- *Always follow instructions.*

KETTLE DESCALER: *Dip-It.* From hardware stores.

- *Always follow instructions.*

LEATHER SHOE POLISH: *Kiwi, Esquire.* From supermarkets.

- *Always follow instructions.*

IGHTER FLUID: *Ronsonal, Penn Champ.* rom supermarkets and hardware stores. Use ndiluted. Inflammable.
- Never use on acetate, triacetate, modacrylic r rayon fabrics.
- Always test first.

INSEED OIL: From art stores.

IALT VINEGAR: *Heinz.* From supermarkets. Ise full strength or diluted with water.

IARBLE CLEANER: *Marble Magic.* From ardware stores.
- Always follow instructions

IETAL CLEANER: *Instant Dip* (silver), *Aluinum Jelly* (aluminum), *Brasso* (copper, brass). rom supermarkets and hardware stores.
- Always follow instructions.

IETAL POLISH: *Noxon, Twinkle, Goddard's ong Term Brass and Copper Polish, Goddard's ilow.* From supermarkets and hardware stores.
- Always follow instructions

IAIL POLISH REMOVER: *Cutex, Revlon.* rom supermarkets and drugstores. Use full rength. Inflammable. Poisonous.
- Never use on acetate, triacetate, modacrylic r rayon fabrics.

IIL STAIN REMOVER: *Asta.* From hardware ores.
- Always follow instructions

IVEN CLEANER: *Easy Off* (aerosol, spray), fr. Muscle (spray), *Dew.* From supermarkets.
- Always follow instructions

IXALIC ACID CRYSTALS: From hardware ores.
- Always follow instructions
- Always test first.

IAINT BRUSH CLEANER: *UGL.* From hard- are stores. Inflammable.
- Never use on acetate, triacetate, modacrylic r rayon fabrics.
- Always follow instructions
- Always test first.

IAINT REMOVER: *Red Devil, Zip Strip.* From ardware stores.
- Always follow instructions

IARAFFIN: From hardware stores. Poisonous nd inflammable.

IICTURE CLEANER: From art stores.
- Never use on valuable paintings.
- Always follow instructions

IRE-WASH PRODUCTS: *Shout, Spray N' Iash, Grease Relief, Axion.* From supermarkets. Ise on washable colorfast fabrics on grease and esh stains before washing.
- Always follow manufacturer's instructions.

IUMICE STONE: From drugstores.

IUST REMOVER: *Liquid Wrench, Rust Jelly, aval Jelly.* From hardware stores.
- Always follow instructions

IAND: From builders' supply stores.

SCOURING PADS: *Ajax, Brillo, Scotch Brite, Dobie, S.O.S., Rescue II, Scrubbie.* From super- markets.
- Always follow instructions

SHELLAC SOLVENT (METHYLATED SPI- RITS): From hardware and building supply stores.

SLATE CLEANER: *Marble Magic.* From hard- ware stores.
- Always follow instructions

SOAP: *Ivory, Lux, Lava.* From supermarkets.

SPIRIT OF SALTS: From hardware stores. Highly corrosive.

SUEDE CLEANER: *Lady Esquire, Renuzit.* From shoe repair and hardware stores.
- Always follow instructions

TILE BLEACH: From building supply stores. Toxic.
- Always follow instructions.

TILE POLISH: *Hercules.* From hardware stores.
- Always follow instructions.

TOILET BOWL CLEANERS: *Vanish, Sani- Flush.* From supermarkets.
- Never use with bleach.
- Always follow instructions

TURPENTINE: From hardware stores. Inflam- mable.
- Never use on acetate, triacetate, modacrylic or rayon fabrics.
- Always test first.

TURPENTINE SUBSTITUTE: *Turpeline.* Any weak-strength replacements for turpentine. From hardware stores.

UPHOLSTERY SHAMPOO: *Glamorine, Bis- sell Upholstery Shampoo.* From hardware stores.
- Always follow instructions

UPHOLSTERY SPOTTING KIT: *KR-2.* From hardware stores.

VINEGAR: See White vinegar and Malt vinegar.

VINYL UPHOLSTERY CLEANER: *Turtle Upholstery Cleaner, Armor All.* From hardware stores and car accessory stores.
- Always follow instructions

WASHING SODA: *Arm and Hammer Washing Soda, Elco.* From supermarkets and hardware stores.
- Always follow instructions

WATER SOFTENER: *Calgon.* From super- markets.
- Always follow instructions

WHITE VINEGAR (DILUTE ACETIC ACID): From supermarkets. If color is affected, use ammonia solution 1 tablespoon ammonia to 1 pint water. White vinegar or lemon juice can be used to counteract discoloration from ammonia or other mild alkalies.

WHITING: From artist's supply stores.
- Always follow instructions

WOOD BLEACH: *Mex.* From hardware stores.

- Always follow instructions

WOOLITE: From supermarkets. Use for hand- washing colorfast woolens and other delicate items.

3

ACRYLIC UTENSILS

General stains: Wipe immediately with damp cloth.
Stubborn stains: Use all-purpose cleaner or moistened bicarbonate of soda.
• *Never use harsh abrasives.*
• *Always act fast.*
See also Plastic Furniture (p. 15).

CHINA

Coffee/tea: Rub with moistened bicarbonate of soda or use tea and coffee stain remover.
Egg: Wash immediately in cold water. If necessary, rub with moistened salt.
General stains: Use warm mild detergent solution. Rinse.
• *Never use scouring pads, harsh abrasives, bleach.*
• *Always dry with soft tea towel. Always wash immediately after use.*

COOKING RANGES, GAS AND ELECTRIC

General stains: Wipe with warm liquid dishwashing solution.
Stubborn stains: Use liquid all-purpose cleaner. Use nylon mesh pad if essential. See also Stainless Steel (p. 6) and Enamel (p. 8).
• *Always follow manufacturer's instructions. Always wipe up spills and splashes immediately. Always turn electricity off before cleaning. Always check that gas pilot lights are lit after cleaning.*

CROCKERY

Coffee/tea: Rub with vinegar and salt or rub with moistened bicarbonate of soda or use tea and coffee stain remover.
Cracked crockery: Boil in a pan of milk for 45 minutes.
Grease: Add a few tablespoons of vinegar to dishwashing liquid.
See also Earthenware.

CRYSTAL/CUT GLASS, including chandeliers

General stains: Rinse in 1 to 3 vinegar and warm water solution. Air dry.
Chandeliers: Use ammonia solution plus dishwashing liquid. Wear cotton gloves. Dip hands in solution and rub crystal clean.
• *Never put crystal or cut glass in the dishwasher.*

CUTLERY

See Knives and Silver, Stainless Steel (p. 9).

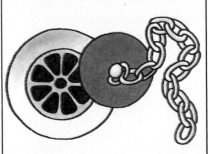

DRAINS

Grease-blocked: Pour 1 quart boiling water plus handful washing soda down outlet. Or use cup of salt and cup of bicarbonate of soda followed by boiling water.
Bad Blockage: Use drain cleaner or call plumber.

EARTHENWARE

Burned-on food: Soak until loose. Wash.
• *Never place in hot water when cold, or vice-versa. Never soak for long.*
• *Always follow manufacturer's cleaning instructions if available.*

FREEZERS

See Refrigerators (p. 6).

GILT AND SILVER ORNAMENTED GLASS

• *Never use very hot soapy water or soak for long. Never use ammonia, washing soda or harsh soaps. Never put in dishwater.*
• *Always use detergent.*

GLASS, including carafes and decanters

Interior sediment stains: Soak container for two days in distilled water. Wash. If necessary, repeat, adding lemon juice or vinegar to distilled water.
Stubborn interior stains: Swill with vinegar and sand or cooking salt.
Grease: Wipe with shellac solvent.
General stains: Wash in warm liquid dishwashing solution. If glass has been discolored due to bad storage, add 1 tablespoon ammonia. Rinse.
• *Always rinse well.*

See also Cooking Ranges, Crystal (p. 4), Heat-Resistant Cooking Glass (below), Mirrors (p. 5), Windows (p. 6) and Glass Tables (p. 14).

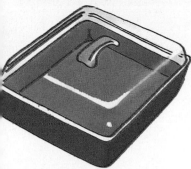

HEAT-RESISTANT COOKING GLASS (Pyrex)

Burned-on food: Soak in warm liquid dishwashing solution.

Grease: Soak in mild ammonia solution. Wash.

Sugar/starch: Soak in solution of 3 tablespoons bicarbonate of soda to 1 quart of warm water. Wash.

● *Never put pans on direct flame or heat.*
● *Always rinse well.*

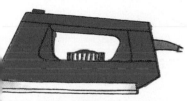

IRONS, PRESSING (Non-steam)

Melted nylon: Heat iron and scrape off with wood spatula.

General stains: *Aluminum soleplate:* Use fine steel wool or abrasive powder or use iron cleaner. *Non-stick soleplate:* Use soapy sponge or nylon mesh pad.

● *Never use abrasives near chromium plating or non-stick surfaces.*
● *Always check manufacturer's cleaning instructions.*

IRONS, PRESSING (Steam)

Burned-on spots: Rub with hot salt and vinegar solution.

Scale deposits: Use coffee and tea kettle destainer or consult professionals.

Wax build-up: 1. Rub with very fine sandpaper. 2. Polish with fine steel wool. 3. Wipe with damp cloth.

General stains: See Non-steam Irons (above).

Never/Always: See Non-steam Irons (above).

KETTLES (Exteriors)

See Metals (pp. 8-9).

● *Always unplug electric kettles before cleaning. Always follow manufacturer's cleaning instructions.*

KETTLES (Interiors)

Scale deposits: Use kettle destainer or boil kettle with a 1 to 1 vinegar to water solution. Leave overnight. Rinse well.

● *Always follow manufacturer's cleaning instructions.*

KNIVES (Carbon steel blades)

General stains: Rub with nylon scouring pad.

Stubborn stains: Polish blade with abrasive powder on the end of a cork. Or use wet and dry abrasive paper.

● *Never soak in water or put in the dishwasher.*
● *Always dry thoroughly immediately after washing.*

See also Stainless Steel (p. 9)

KNIVES (Horn, bone or ivory handles)

General stains: Use warm soapy water.

● *Never soak in water.*

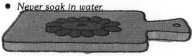

MELAMINE TABLEWARE/ FORMICA

Coffee/tea: Use sterilizing agent or rub with bicarbonate of soda. *Or* fill with hot water and add denture cleaning tablets. Leave one hour. Wash.

Stubborn stains: Use Formica cleaner.

● *Never use abrasive cleaners. Never put near direct flame.*
● *Always wash immediately.*

MIRRORS

Hair Spray: Use shellac solvent then glass cleaner.

General stains: Wash with mild vinegar, ammonia solution, cool tea or glass cleaner.

Stubborn stains: Wash with mild borax solution.

● *Never wet the backing.*
● *Always buff with a soft cloth.*

MOTHER-OF-PEARL HANDLES

General stains: Use paste of powdered whiting and water. Rub on gently. Wash off with warm soapy water. *Or* use non-abrasive liquid furniture polish.

Stubborn stains: Consult professionals.

● *Never use ammonia. Never soak in water or put in dishwasher.*

OVENS

General stains: Wipe with warm liquid dishwashing solution or use liquid all-purpose cleaner.

Stubborn stains: Use oven cleaner *or* 1. Heat oven. 2. Switch off. 3. Leave one pint hot water plus two tablespoons ammonia inside overnight. 4. Air. Then wash with warm soapy water.

Glass doors: Rub with bicarbonate of soda or use washing soda or use liquid all-purpose cleaner.

● *Never use abrasives on non-stick surfaces. Never use aerosol oven cleaner on warm glass.*
● *Always follow manufacturer's instructions. Always check that cleaner is suitable for vitreous enamel oven linings.*

See also Ranges (p. 4).

PORCELAIN

See China (p. 4).

POTS AND PANS

See Metals (pp. 8-9).

REFRIGERATORS/FREEZERS

General stains: *Exteriors:* Use warm detergent solution. Rub dry.
Interiors: Use moistened bicarbonate of soda.
- *Never use abrasives.*
- *Always dry well.*

SILVER CUTLERY

See Silver (p. 9)

SINKS, STAINLESS STEEL

Rust: Rub with lighter fluid. Clean as usual.
Water spots: Rub with white vinegar or shellac solvent. Rinse immediately.
General Stains: Use dishwashing liquid.
- *Never use harsh abrasives, scouring pads, salt, vinegar, steel wool or undissolved detergent powder.*
- *Always rinse and dry after use.*
See also Stainless Steel (p. 9).

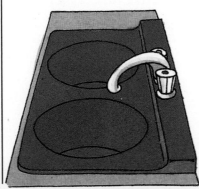

SINKS, VITREOUS OR PORCELAIN ENAMELED

Blue/green drip stains: Use a vitreous enamel cleaner or soapsuds plus ammonia.
Hard water marks: See drip stains, repeat if necessary.
Rust: See drip stains, or use a bath stain remover with rust-removing properties. Rub light stains with a cut lemon. Rub stubborn stains with borax and lemon juice paste.
Stubborn stains: 1. Rub with bleach solution or apply paste of cream of tartar and dilute hydrogen peroxide. 2. Scrub. 3. If necessary, add 2 drops of ammonia to paste. Leave 2 hours. 4. Scrub and rinse.
- *Never use harsh abrasives or strong bleaches.*
- *Always rinse well after use. Always clean fixtures according to the material of which they are made.*

TAPS

- *Never use abrasives.*
See also Chrome-plating (p. 8), Gold (p. 8).

TEAPOTS

See Aluminum (p. 8), Silver (p. 9).

THERMOS FLASK CONTAINERS

Coffee/tea: Put crushed eggshells inside with a little hot water. Shake well. Wash. *Or* use tea and coffee stain remover.
General stains: Fill with warm water and 1 tablespoon bicarbonate of soda. Leave three hours. Wash.
- *Never immerse entire bottle in water.*
- *Always rinse well.*

WALL TILES

General stains: *Aluminum:* Wipe with hot liquid dishwashing solution. See also Aluminum (p. 8).
Ceramic: See Ceramic Tiles (p. 10).
Mirrored: See Mirrors (p. 5).

WINDOWS

Paint: If fresh, use turpentine, liquid dry-cleaner, or nail polish remover. If dried, soften with turpentine. Scrape off.
Putty: Use ammonia or soften with turpentine. Scrape off.
General stains: See Mirrors.
- *Never scrub dirty glass with dry cloth. Never clean windows when the sun is shining or in frosty weather.*

SHOWER CURTAINS

Mildew: Wipe with weak bleach solution. Wash.
General stains: Sponge with soapsuds or mild detergent. Rinse. Air dry.
● *Never rub, squeeze or wring plastic or rubber shower curtains.*
● *Always test first. Always follow manufacturer's care instructions.*

SINKS, FIRECLAY

General stains: Use bathroom cleaner.
Stubborn stains: Use abrasive powder or line sink with paper towels and saturate with bleach. Leave for 30 minutes. Remove. Rinse.

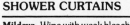

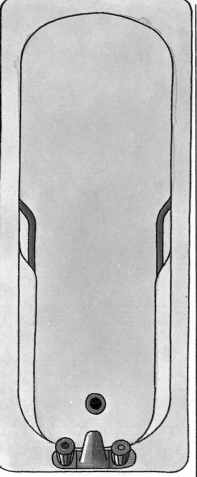

LAVATORY/TOILET BOWL

Calcium rings: Gently rub with fine pumice stone or abrasive paper.
General stains: *Bowl:* Apply paste of borax and lemon juice, bleach or bathroom cleaner to wet surface. Leave 2 hours. Scrub.
Seat: Clean regularly with warm water and disinfectant.
● *Never mix cleaning agents.*

BATHS, ACRYLIC/FIBERGLASS

Grease: Use warm washing soda solution.
Light scratches: Rub with silver metal polish.
General stains: Wipe with dishwashing liquid or soap.
Stubborn stains: 1. Gently rub with progressively finer wet abrasive paper until surface is smooth. 2. Rub with silver metal polish.
● *Never use bath-foam, bath-cubes etc. Never use harsh abrasives or any abrasives on glass fiber.*
● *Always rinse well after use.*

BATHS, VITREOUS/ PORCELAIN ENAMELED

Rings: Wash off with dishwashing liquid.
Yellowed bathtub: Rub with salt and turpentine solution.
General stains: Use bathroom cleaner.
● *Never use harsh abrasives or strong bleaches.*
● *Always rinse well after use. Always clean fixtures according to the material from which they are made.*

WALL TILES

Mirrored: See Mirrors (p. 5).
See also Wall Tiles Kitchens (p. 6).

METALS, GENERAL

- *Never use harsh abrasives.*
- *Always identify metal before cleaning. If in doubt, use a metal polish for soft metals.*

ALUMINUM (pots and pans)

Burned-on food: Fill pan with water. Boil. Scrape with wooden spoon. Wash.
General stains: Soak in solution 1 tablespoon borax to 1 pint hot water. Wash as usual.
Stubborn stains: Simmer strong solution of cream of tartar or vinegar for 20 minutes. Wash.
Teapots: **General stains:** Fill with water and 2 teaspoons borax. Leave 2 hours. Wash.
- *Never put colored aluminum in dishwasher. Never treat non-stick or mirrored finishes with abrasive cleaners or sharp implements. Never use washing soda. Never store food in aluminum.*
- *Always clean with soap-filled pad rubbing in one direction only. Always rinse thoroughly.* See also Metal Furniture (p. 14), Wall Tiles (p. 6).

BRASS

Corrosion: Boil small objects in water containing salt and vinegar. Then use brass metal polish.
Tarnished: See Copperware (column 3).
General stains: Use brass polish or mix polish with lemon juice. See Copperware (column 3).
Stubborn stains: Clean with strong ammonia solution. Polish.
Brass fire tools: Rub with fine steel wool in one direction only. Polish.
- *Always consult professionals on antique pieces.*

BRONZE

Green spots/Verdigris: Rub with brown leather polish. Buff. *Or* brush with stiff brush then swab with 10% vinegar solution. Rinse, dry, buff and polish.

General stains: *Lacquered bronze:* If cracked or peeling, re-lacquer.
Unlacquered bronze: Wash with mild soap or detergent solution. *Or* wash with hot vinegar or buttermilk. Rinse. Polish.
Stubborn stains: Wash in hot soapy water, *or* rub with pure turpentine *or* rub with paraffin. When dry, brush with stiff brush. Polish.
- *Never use wire brush or harsh abrasives.*
- *Always consult professionals on antique pieces.*

CAST IRON, POTS AND PANS (uncoated)

Burned-on food: Fill pan with water and a little washing soda. Boil. Wash.
Rust: Use steel wool and abrasive powder.
Stubborn stains: Use steel wool or scouring pad.
- *Never use synthetic detergents. Never store pans with lids on.*
- *Always rinse and dry well. Always coat thinly with oil before storing.*

CAST IRON, POTS AND PANS (coated)

If coated with enamel, see Enamelware (column 3). If non-stick, see Non-Stick Pots and Pans (p. 9).

CHROMIUM-PLATING

Grease: Apply moistened bicarbonate of soda. *Or* use whiting or chrome metal polish.
Green spots/corrosion: Use chrome metal polish for mild corrosion. Replace or replate badly corroded taps, pipes, etc.
General stains: Wash with warm, soapy water. Dry. *Or* use ammonia or chrome metal polish.
- *Never use abrasives.*
- *Always use cleaning agents sparingly.*

COPPERWARE

Green stains: Use soapsuds plus a few drops of ammonia.
Tarnished: Rub with a cut lemon dipped in salt or use copper metal polish.
General stains: Rub with paste of vinegar, salt and flour. Wash.
- *Always wash thoroughly after using acids or polishes.*

ENAMELWARE

Burned-on food: Fill pan with cold water plus 2 teaspoons bicarbonate of soda. Boil. Wash.
Grease stains: Use all-purpose cleaner.
General stains: Rub with moistened bicarbonate of soda or soak in hot detergent solution or use an all-purpose cleaner.
Stubborn stains: Fill pan with cold water plus 1 teaspoon bleach. Leave 3 hours. Wash.
- *Never use harsh abrasives. Never use to store acidic foods.*

GOLD

Tarnished: Consult professionals.
General stains: Use soft metal polish. Buff.
- *Never clean plated items too often.*

IRON

Rust: Rub with paraffin-moistened steel wool.
Rusty hinges: Lubricate with rust remover.
Stubborn rust stains: If possible, soak in paraffin. Then rub with steel wool. *Or* use rust remover.
See also Irons (p. 5)

JEWELRY

- *Always treat carefully. Consult professionals if necessary.*

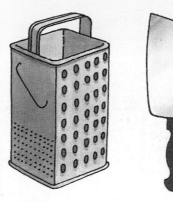

~EAD

~hite deposits: 1. If possible, boil in several ~anges of water. 2. Place in 1 part of vinegar ~ 9 parts water. 3. Rinse in water plus 1 ~aspoon bicarbonate of soda. 4. Rinse in dis~led water.
~eneral stains: Scrub with turpentine.
~tubborn stains: Use abrasive powder.

~ICKEL

~eneral stains: Use whiting/fine abrasive pow~er moistened with alcohol. Wash. Rinse, buff. ~r use metal polish.
● *Always clean frequently.*

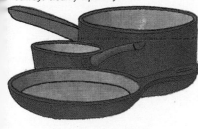

~NON-STICK POTS AND PANS

General stains: Follow manufacturer's instruc~tions.
Stubborn stains: Boil solution of 1 cup water, 2 teaspoons bicarbonate of soda and ½ cup bleach in pan for 5 – 10 minutes. Wash.
● *Never use abrasives.*
● *Always dry well and lightly oil before storing.*

PEWTER OR BRITANNIA METAL

Grease: Rub with shellac solvent. Wash.
General stains: Wash with soapy water. Dry. Or Rub with cabbage leaf.
Stubborn stains: Rub with fine steel wool and olive oil. Or rub with paste of mild abrasive powder and olive oil. Or consult professionals.

SILVER AND SILVERPLATE, including cutlery

Egg stains: Rub with table salt.
Food stains: Wash immediately after use. Dry.
General stains: Use silver metal polish or use moistened cigarette ash. Wash, rinse and dry.
Teapots: Place 1 tablespoon washing soda plus several bits of foil in teapot. Fill with boiling water. Leave 1 hour. Rinse.
● *Never bring silver into contact with rubber. Never use abrasives or bleach. Never wrap in newspaper. Never clean on stainless steel sink.*
● *Always wash before and after polishing. Always dry thoroughly immediately after washing. Always store carefully.*
See also Candle Holders (p. 16).

STAINLESS STEEL, including cutlery, pots and pans

Rings around edge: Use shellac solvent. Wash thoroughly.
Burned-on food: Use mild abrasive cleaner or scouring pad.
General stains: Wash with hot soapy water. Or use stainless steel metal polish.
Teapots: Fill with boiling water plus 1 tablespoon washing soda. Leave 1 hour. Rinse.
● *Never use harsh abrasives, bleach, salt or silver dip. Never get near direct flame or soak in vinegar or other food acids.*
● *Always wash promptly after use. Always rinse well. Always avoid hot grease splashes.*
See also Knives (p. 5) and Sinks (p. 6).

STEEL

Burned-on food: Fill pan with liquid dishwashing solution. Boil. Wash as usual.
Rust stains: Use rust remover.
General stains: Use abrasive powder, fine steel wool or medium grade emery cloth. Wash. Dry.
● *Never bring into contact with acids or water for long periods of time. Never put hot pans into liquid dishwashing solution without cooling first.*
● *Always protect your eyes when cleaning steel. Always dry steel pots and pans well and lightly oil before storing.*

TINNED WARE

Grease: Wash in hot washing soda solution. Rinse.
Rust: Rub with potato dipped in mild abrasive powder. Wash.
General stains: Wash immediately after use in hot liquid dishwashing solution. Rinse.
Stubborn stains: Boil item in strong washing soda solution. Wash.
● *Never use harsh abrasives.*
● *Always dry thoroughly.*
See also Carbon Steel Knives (p. 4) and Metal Furniture (p. 14).

ZINC

Tarnish: Rub with vinegar or lemon juice solution. Leave 5 minutes. Rinse, dry and polish.
General stains: Use hot soapy water.
Stubborn stains: Use mild abrasive powder.

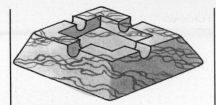

ALABASTER

Nicotine stains: Wipe with turpentine. Buff.
General stains: Use dishwashing solution.
Stubborn stains: Consult professionals.
● *Never immerse in water.*

ASPHALT, BITUMASTIC, MASTIC, PITCHMASTIC, SEMASTIC, THERMOPLASTIC

General stains: Rub lightly with wire wool. Rinse. Polish.
● *Never use wax polish.*

BRICKWORK (calcium silicate and clay)

Burn marks: Wash with malt vinegar.
Lichens and mosses: Use weed killer. Growth indicates dampness. Treat.
Rust and Iron: Wash with solution of 1 part oxalic acid to 10 parts water.
Tar: 1. Remove excess, unless liable to damage bricks. 2. Scrub with detergent solution. 3. If necessary, sponge with paraffin.
Timber (brown or grey stains): Scrub with solution of 1 part oxalic acid to 40 parts hot water.
● *Never use soap. Never apply chemicals directly.*
● *Always test first. Leave 1 week before proceeding. Always consult professionals for large areas of cleaning and before cleaning Calcium Silicate brickwork, especially if using acids. Always saturate with clean water before and after using chemicals. Always wear protective clothing and ensure good ventilation.*

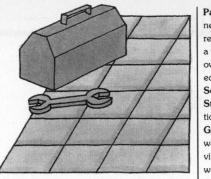

CEMENT, CONCRETE AND STONE

Coffee/tea: Scrub with hot soapy water or apply bleach solution. Rinse.
Ink: Apply bleach solution.
Oil/grease: Scrub with heavy detergent solution or slate cleaner. Rinse. Or sprinkle with an absorbent powder. After a while, sweep up.
Paint (emulsion): Rub with acetone.
Paint (oil): Use paint remover. Follow manufacturer's instructions.
Rust: Use rust remover or concrete cleaner. Follow manufacturer's instructions.
Timber (yellow/brown): Scrub vigorously with bleach solution. Rinse.
General stains: Scrub with detergent of washing soda solution.
Stubborn stains: Repeat as above. Or scrub with strong bleach solution.
● *Never use soap or scouring powder. Never use acid or limestone.*
● *Always scrape off or mop up deposit before applying chemicals. Always rinse with clear water after treatment.*

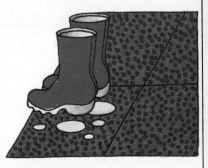

CERAMIC (Glazed) AND TERRAZZO TILES

Cloudy film on surface: Use water softener.
Iron: Use abrasive powder.
Lime: Apply full-strength vinegar. Leave 10 minutes. Wash.
Paint: 1. Wipe immediately and scour. 2. If necessary, use commercial tile bleach or paint remover. Test first. Follow instructions. Or place a thick cloth saturated with hydrogen peroxide over stain. Cover first cloth with cloth moistened with ammonia. Repeat if necessary.
Soap scum: Use paraffin.
Stains between tiles: Brush with bleach solution or re-grout.
General stains: Use mild detergent solution or wash with solution of ½ cup ammonia, ½ cup vinegar, ¼ washing soda and 1 gallon warm water.
Stubborn stains: 1. See General Stains (above), or scrub with paste of bicarbonate of soda and bleach. Or consult professionals.
● *Never apply a damp cloth to tiles while hot or if near a fire. Never use acid solution or harsh abrasives on tiles.*
● *Always rinse thoroughly.*

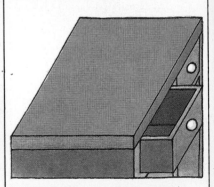

CORK TILES

See Plastic Films/Seals (p. 11) and Cork (p. 12).

ENAMEL

See Enamelware (p. 8).

LAMINATED PLASTIC (Arborite, Formica, Melamine-faced chipboard, PVC, Warerite)

Coffee, fruit juices, hair-dye, iodine, nail-

polish remover, tea, red wine: Mop up immediately with hot soapy water.

Food and ink: Rub in full-strength dishwashing liquid or liquid all-purpose cleaner.

Stubborn stains: Wash with hot soapy water or apply paste of bicarbonate of soda and water. Rub off after 2 minutes.

- *Never use abrasives.*
- *Always mop stains up quickly.*

LEATHER DESKTOPS

See Leather (pp. 16-17).

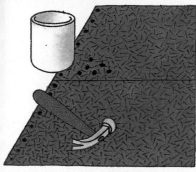

LINOLEUM

Crayon: Rub with silver metal polish.
Scuff marks: Rub with floor polish emulsion.
General stains: Use all-purpose cleaner or washing soda solution.

- *Never use harsh soaps or scouring powders. Never leave oil or water standing on linoleum. Dry well after washing.*

MARBLE

Cosmetics, foliage, non-metalic ink, tea, tobacco: Apply hydrogen peroxide solution plus a few drops of ammonia. Leave 2 hours. Rinse. Dry.
Grease, oil: Rub with alcohol/acetone/lighter fluid. Rinse. Dry.
Rust: Use rust remover. Rinse. Dry.
Wine, coffee, alcohol, spirits, cigarette burns: Consult professionals.

General stains: Use liquid abrasive cleaner/lemon juice/vinegar. Rinse. Dry.
Stubborn stains: As above. Or apply a paste of marble cleaner and water. Rinse off when dry.

- *Never use heavy detergents, acids, gasoline, paraffin or turpentine substitute.*
- *Always wipe spills immediately with warm soapy water. Always rinse well and buff with soft cloth. Always consult professionals for antique marble or if very stained.*

ONYX

General stains: Use liquid dishwashing solution.
Stubborn stains: Wipe with shellac solvent or consult professionals.

- *Never immerse in water.*
- *Always wipe spills immediately. Always handle as little as possible.*

PLASTIC FILMS/SEALS

Dull-looking: Rub in toothpaste. Buff.
Watermarks: Rub with liquid floor wax polish.
General stains: Clean with liquid abrasive cleaner or detergent.

- *Never cut on surface. Never use abrasives or wire wool. Never put extreme heat on surface.*
- *Always wipe spills immediately.*

QUARRY TILES

White patches: Wash with 1 tablespoon vinegar to 1 pint water solution. Do not rinse. Repeat if necessary.
General stains: Mop with liquid abrasive cleaner solution.

RUBBER

Scuff marks: Rub with abrasive cleaner. Rinse.
General stains: Wash with soapy water. Rinse.

- *Never put anything hot on rubber. Never use detergent, gasoline, paraffin, wax polish, or turpentine substitute. Never wash unless necessary.*
- *Always remove fat, grease, oil, gasoline, turpentine and fruit juices immediately.*

SLATE

Grease: Use oil stain remover.
General stains: Use washing soda solution. Rinse.
Stubborn stains: Repeat as above or use slate cleaner.

- *Always rinse well.*

TERRAZZO TILES

See Ceramic Tiles (p. 10).

VINYL/VINYL ASBESTOS

Scuff marks: Use soft pencil eraser or use floor polish emulsion.
General stains: Use warm soapy water and rub gently with wire wool. If necessary, add all-purpose cleaner.

- *Never use gasoline, paraffin, lighter fluid, turpentine, or wax polish.*
- *Always check manufacturer's care instructions. Always rinse well.*

See also Vinyl Upholstery (p. 27) and Vinyl Wallcoverings (p. 12).

WOODEN FLOORS/ WORK SURFACES

General stains: *Untreated wood:* Use detergent and as little water as possible. Or scrub with scouring powder.
Painted wood: Wash with liquid dishwashing solution or use hot water plus 1 teaspoon washing soda per gallon water. Rinse.
Sealed/varnished wood: Rub with cold tea or use liquid abrasive cleaner.
Waxed wood: Use mild detergent solution or fine steel wool dipped in liquid floor/furniture wax. Polish.
White spots and rings: Rub with wood ash and raw potato or salad oil. Or rub with moistened cigarette ash or mayonnaise.

- *Never over-wet. Never use abrasives.*
- *Always wipe up spills immediately.*

See also Wooden Furniture (p. 15) and Painted Wood (p. 13).

BRICKWALLS (Calcium Silicate and clay)

Efflorescence (white crystals/scale deposit): Wash repeatedly with water. Let bricks dry between washings. Or brush wall when most efflorescent. (Not sandfaced bricks.) Never let salt accumulate at foot of wall. To prevent recurrence, professionals often use muriatic acid.

Lime and mortar: If possible, scrape away. Wash.

Oil: Sponge with turpentine substitute.

Paint (graffiti): 1. Use paint remover. When soft, scrape off. 2. Wash with soapy water. 3. If necessary, grind off face of calcium silicate brickwork.

Rust and Iron: Wash with solution of 1 part oxalic acid to 10 parts water.

Smoke and soot: Rub with art gum eraser or scrub with detergent.

Clay brickwork: Use solution of 1 part spirit of salts and 6 parts water (highly corrosive). Never allow near mortar. See also Brickwork (p. 10).

BURLAP

See Hessian (column 2)

CORK WALLS

General stains: Sponge gently with warm, mild detergent solution.
- *Never over-wet.*

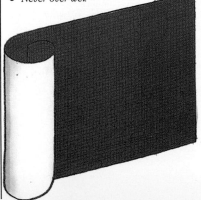

FABRIC WALLCOVERINGS

General stains: Dab with baby powder. Leave 2 hours. Brush off gently.
- *Never use dry-cleaner or upholstery cleaners.*
- *Always follow manufacturer's care instructions.*

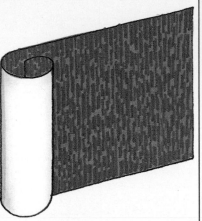

GRASSCLOTH

Grease: Use aerosol dry-cleaner. Follow instructions.

General stains: Dab with baby powder. Leave 2 hours. Brush off gently.
- *Never use water.*
- *Always test first.*

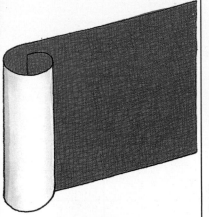

HESSIAN (BURLAP)

Grease: See Grasscloth (above).

General stains: Dab with baby powder. Leave 2 hours. Brush off gently or rub with stale white bread.
- *Never use water.*
- *Always test first.*

PAINTED WALLS AND CEILINGS (water-based paint)

General stains: Dust. Wash with mild solution of dishwashing liquid. Work from bottom up. Clean small areas at a time. Rinse and dry before cleaning next area.

Stubborn stains: Use mild detergent solution as above.
- *Never use washing or scouring powders.*
- *Always use clean water and rinse thoroughly. Always turn electricity off at the fusebox.*

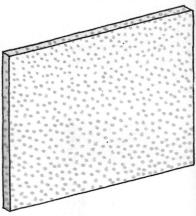

POLYSTYRENE (expanded)

General stains: Sponge with warm mild detergent solution. Rinse.
- *Never use anything stronger than above. Never apply pressure.*
- *Always leave to dry thoroughly.*

VINYL WALLCOVERINGS

Ballpoint ink: Wash immediately with warm soap or detergent solution.

Candle wax: 1. Lift off carefully when hard. 2. Dab remaining color gently with shellac

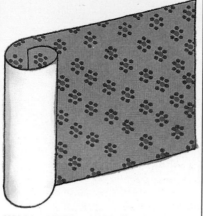

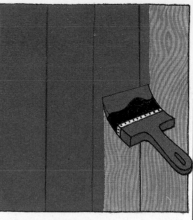

solvent. 3. If necessary, finish with all-purpose cleaner.

Crayon: Wipe with damp cloth, then all-purpose cleaner or silver metal polish.

Felt-tip pen: Use all-purpose cleaner, full strength dishwashing liquid or shellac solvent.

Hair oil: Rub lightly with all-purpose cleaner or turpentine substitute.

General stains: See Painted Walls (p. 12).

● *Never over-wet. Never use ammonia, acetone, abrasives or nail-polish remover.*

● *Always work from bottom up.*

See also Vinyl Flooring (p. 11) and Vinyl Upholstery (p. 27).

WALL-HANGINGS, SILK

● *Always consult professionals*

Also see silk (p. 18).

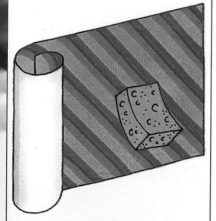

WALLPAPER, WASHABLE

● *Never over-wet.*

● *Always test first.*

See also Painted Walls (p. 12).

WALLPAPER, NON-WASHABLE

Candle wax: Draw out grease with warm iron on blotting paper over stain, then use dry-cleaner solution. Occasionally traces left.

Crayon: 1. Sponge lightly with liquid dry-cleaner solution. 2. Remove residue as for candle wax (above) or rub gently with moistened bicarbonate of soda.

Food/grease stains: 1. Draw out grease with warm iron on blotting paper over stain. Or apply paste of absorbent powder and dry-cleaning fluid. Brush off when dry. 2. If necessary, rub stain with moistened borax.

Ink: Blot immediately. Do not smear. Then use ink eradicator. Test first.

Lipstick: Use dry-cleaner solution. Occasionally traces left.

Pencil marks/light smudges: Use an eraser.

Adhesive tape: Remove. Draw out mark with warm iron on blotting paper over stain.

General stains: Rub over with stale white bread.

● *Never use water.*

● *Always test first.*

WALLPAPER, TEXTURED AND EMBOSSED

Grease: Dab with baby powder. Leave 2 hours. Brush off gently.

General stains: Sponge with mild detergent solution.

● *Never press hard. Never overwet.*

● *Always test first.*

WHITEWASHED WALLS

● *Always repaint when stained.*

WOOD, PAINTED (oil-based paint)

Grease: Use mild detergent solution or all-purpose cleaner.

General stains: Use a paintwork cleaner. *Or* wash with hot, mild washing soda solution. *Or* use liquid dishwashing solution.

● *Never use abrasives.*

● *Always work from bottom up.*

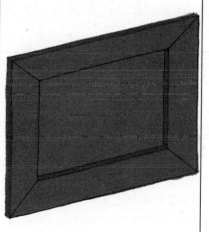

WOOD, PANELING

Fine scratches: Rub with fine steel wool and turpentine substitute. Rub in direction of the grain. Polish. Buff.

General stains: *Sealed:* Wash with mild detergent solution. Rinse. Buff.

Wax-finished: Use furniture cleaner.

FURNITURE, GENERAL

- *Always follow manufacturer's instructions with modern furniture. Always consult professionals with antique furniture. Always identify surfaces before cleaning.*

Furniture

ANTIQUE WOOD

Grease: 1. Rub with chamois leather and solution 1 part vinegar to 8 parts water. Dry. Buff. 2. Polish as usual.
General stains: Consult professionals.
- *Never use modern furniture polishes with added silicones.*

BAMBOO FURNITURE

General stains: Scrub gently with warm soapy water plus a little borax. Rinse with salt water.
- *Never use detergent.*

BASKETWARE AND CANE FURNITURE

General stains: *Varnished furniture:* Wipe with damp cloth or use mild soapsuds plus a little ammonia. Rinse. Dry.
Unvarnished furniture: 1. Scrub lightly with warm salt water or rub with fine steel wool and mild washing soda solution. 2. Rinse with cold water. Dry.
- *Never over-wet cane.*
- *Always rinse well with cold water.*

FRENCH POLISHED WOOD

Alcohol: Wipe up immediately.
Heat/water marks: Rub with solution ¼ pint turpentine and 1 pint linseed oil. Leave 8 hours. Remove and polish. *Or see White Rings below.*
Scratches: Rub with furniture renovator in direction of grain or use commercial high gloss polish following instructions carefully.
White heat marks: May need to be stripped down and re-polished. Consult professionals.
White rings: Saturate cotton wool pad with shellac solvent. Place inside soft white cloth. Carefully rub quickly over surface.
General stains: Rub with solution 1 part white vinegar to 8 parts water. Dry well and polish.
Stubborn stains: Consult professionals.
- *Never place hot or wet things directly onto surface.*
- *Always consult professionals, especially if antique furniture.*

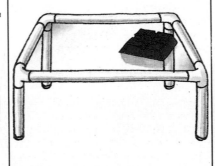

GLASS TABLE TOPS

General stains: 1. Rub with lemon juice or alcohol. 2. Dry with paper towel. 3. Buff with newspaper. *Or use glass/window cleaner. See also Kitchen Windows (p. 6).*

LAMPSHADES

General stains: *Buckram:* Rub with turpentine.
Fiberglass: Wipe with damp cloth.
Hand-painted silk, linen or chintz: Consult professionals.
Imitation parchment: Use paste furniture polish or rub with India rubber.
Metallic paper: Rub with 1 tablespoon turpentine plus ½ cup paraffin. Wipe off.
Nylon, rayon and silk (detachable shades): 1. Repeatedly dip shade in warm soap/detergent solution. Test first. 2. Rinse in warm water. 3. Dry quickly.
Nylon, rayon and silk (Shade glued to frame): Consult professionals.
Parchment (Vellum): Wipe with solution of 1 tablespoon soapflakes, 1 tablespoon water, 2 tablespoons shellac solvent.
Plastic: Wipe with warm soapy water. Rinse. Pat dry.
- *Always dust shades regularly. Always clean according to surface. Always switch off the light and unplug before cleaning the shade.*

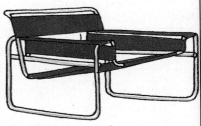

METAL FURNITURE

Aluminum: Use liquid dishwashing solution. Or rub with fine steel wool in one direction only. Or use metal polish.
Grease: Add 1 tablespoon borax to liquid dishwashing solution.
Tubular steel: Use metal polish.
Rust: Rub with turpentine.
See also Metals (p. 8).

PAINTED FURNITURE

See Painted Wood (p. 13).

PLASTIC FURNITURE
(acrylic and polyurethane)

Scratches: 1. Rub acrylics with soft metal polish. 2. Wipe over with moist cloth. Buff.
General stains: *Acrylics:* Rub with liquid abrasive cleaner or acrylic cleaner.
Polyurethane: Rub with liquid dishwashing solution.

- *Never use heavy abrasive cleaners, chemicals, acids, gasoline, undiluted bleach, disinfectant, dry-cleaners or acetone.*
- *Always avoid heat*

WOODEN FURNITURE

Alcohol: Act fast 1. Mop up and rub with palm of hand. 2. Mop with a cloth dampened with a little teak oil furniture polish, or linseed oil. 3. If necessary, rub with paste of oil plus cigarette ash or powdered pumice. 4. Remove and re-wax.
Blood: 1. Mop up. 2. Sandpaper surface lightly. 3. Swab on hydrogen peroxide.
Cigarette burns: 1. Treat as Heat Marks (column 2). 2. If necessary, lightly sandpaper area. 3. Rebuild with plastic wood or colored beeswax.
Dents: 1. Fill hole with hot water. *Or* cover with damp cotton cloth and heat with tip of warm iron. Remove when steaming. 2. When dry, re-wax/polish.
Glue: Rub with cold cream, peanut butter or salad oil.

Grease, fats or oil: Rub with lighter fluid. *Veneered or inlaid wood:* Cover thickly with talcum powder. On top, place few layers of paper tissues. Heat paper with non-steam iron.
Heat marks (white): 1. Remove finish with turpentine substitute. 2. When dry, re-color wood (see Scratches below). 3. Re-polish surface. *Cellulose and lacquered finishes:* 1. Rub with brass metal polish. 2. Remove before dry. 3. Rub with hot polishing cloth (heat with iron). 4. Re-polish.

Oiled wood: Remove finish with turpentine substitute. When dry, if necessary, rub in teak oil furniture polish.
Ink: Wash immediately with water. Then dab with lemon juice.
Paint (oil and water based): *Old stains:* 1. Cover with linseed oil. Leave 1 hour. Scrape off carefully. 2. If necessary, apply paste of oil and powdered pumice. 3. Rub off, wipe with oil. 4. Polish.
Paint (oil based): *Fresh stains:* Wipe with liquid furniture polish or turpentine. Polish.
Paint (water based) *Fresh stains:* Wipe with soap solution.
Paper: To remove, cover with salad oil. Leave 2 hours. Wipe off.
Red Ink stains: 1. See Ink. 2. If necessary, sandpaper wood lightly. Place cotton wool saturated with weak solution of oxalic acid on stain. Leave 2 minutes. Wipe off with damp cloth. 3. Re-polish.

Scratches: Rub wax crayon, shoe polish, or eyebrow pencil into scratch with cotton swab. Match color as closely as possible.

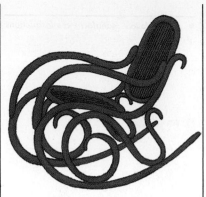

Ebony: Use black.
Mahogany: Use dark brown.
Maple: Use iodine plus alcohol. Dry. Re-wax.
Red mahogany: Apply iodine with fine brush.
Teak: Sandpaper gently. Then rub with solution of equal parts linseed oil and turpentine.
Walnut: Rub with meat of fresh walnut.

Water marks (white): 1. Rub with very fine steel wool and oil in the direction of the grain. Or apply a paste of mayonnaise or olive oil and cigarette ash. 2. Buff with damp cloth. *or* 1. Apply solution of equal parts linseed oil and turpentine. Leave for 2 hours. 2. Remove with vinegar.

Water marks (black): Brush on saturated solution of oxalic acid. Leave 2-3 seconds. Remove with damp cloth. Or rub surface gently with fine steel wool until fresh wood is reached. Re-color or stain wood. See Scratches (column 2). Re-polish or oil.

- *Never use too much water on wood. Never use oiled or treated dust cloths on furniture with waxed surfaces.*

See also Antique Wood (p. 14), French Polished Wood (p. 14) and Painted Wood (p. 13)

ARTIFICIAL FLOWERS (PLASTIC)

General stains: Shake vigorously in salt-filled bag.

BLANKETS

General stains: *Electric blankets:* Follow manufacturer's care instructions. *Synthetic fiber:* Pre-treat spots with heavy-duty liquid detergent. Wash, dry-clean or consult professionals. *Woolen blankets:* Pre-treat spots by softly brushing with warm Woolite solution, dry-clean or consult professionals.

● *Never use soap, very hot water or water softener on untreated wool blankets. Never wash any blankets unless specified by the manufacturer. Never dry-clean electric blankets.*

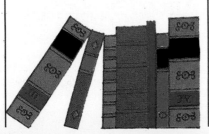

BOOKS

Grease: Rub with soft, white breadcrumbs.
Mildew: Dust with absorbent powder. Leave 2 days. Brush off.
General stains: Use an art gum eraser.
● *Always consult professionals about cleaning valuable books.*
See also Leather (pp. 16-17).

CANDLES

General stains: Sponge with turpentine substitute.

CANDLE HOLDERS

Wax coated: Freeze for 1 hour. Peel wax off. (This does not harm silver.)

CUSHIONS

See Pillows (p. 17)

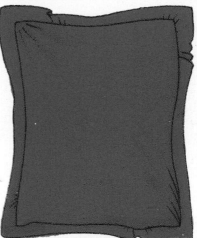

DOWN-FILLED AND CONTINENTAL QUILTS

Act fast. Treat cover according to stain. (See Fabrics (pp. 21-25).
If the filling becomes stained: *Natural fiber fillings:* Dry-clean or consult professionals. *Synthetic fiber fillings:* Machine wash or consult professionals.
● *Never wash too often.*
● *Always follow manufacturer's care instruc-*

tions. *Always use a cover on your down quilt and wash cover according to fabric. Always ensure down quilt is dry before use.*

FOAM RUBBER

See Pillows, Foam. (p. 17).

FRAMES

General stains: *Gilt:* Wipe with a little turpentine, turpentine substitute or use liquid dry-cleaner.
Wood: Wipe with warm soapy water.
● *Never use harsh abrasives.*
● *Always avoid touching the painting.*

IVORY, BONE OR HORN OBJECTS

General stains: Use soft cloth dampened with turpentine substitute.
● *Never use water. Never use turpentine substitute on valuable pieces.*

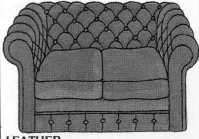

LEATHER

General stains: *Book bindings:* Use leather renovator. Follow instructions. *Clothing/gloves, non-washable:* Consult professionals. *Washable:* Swab with soapy water. Wipe. Dry naturally, Keep gloves on hands and dip into water. Remove to dry.
Desk/table tops: Rub with leather renovator

...after washing.
Ink stains: Rub very gently with a little white spirit.
Luggage/handbags: Rub with eucalyptus oil. Polish with furniture polish.
Shoes: Polish as usual or consult professionals.

Fake leather: Brush gently with warm detergent solution, not soap. Rinse. Buff.
Chamois leather: Wash in warm soapy water. Rinse in warm water plus 1 teaspoon olive oil. Squeeze. Air dry.
Reptile skin: Rub leather renovator in direction of scales.
Suede, non-washable: Consult professionals.
Suede, washable: Follow manufacturer's care instructions, or use suede cleaner.
Suede shoes: Brush gently with warm soapy water. Then with cold water. Dry naturally, or use suede cleaner.
● *Never soak in water (unless chamois). Never use detergent (unless fake leather).*
● *Always follow manufacturer's care instructions.*
See also Upholstery (p. 27).

MATTRESSES

Blood: 1. Tip mattress on side. 2. Sponge with cold, salt water. Rinse with cold water. Or use lather from upholstery cleaner.
Urine: 1. Tip mattress on side. 2. Sponge with cold dishwashing liquid or upholstery shampoo solution. Rinse with cold water plus disinfectant. Or use upholstery spotting kit.
Vomit: 1. Remove deposit. 2. Tip mattress on side. 3. Sponge with warm dishwashing liquid or upholstery shampoo solution. 4. Rinse with warm water plus disinfectant. Blot well.
Stubborn stains: Use soap foam or upholstery shampoo.
● *Never expect miracles. Ring marks may remain after cleaning.*
● *Always follow manufacturer's care instructions. Always clean urine stains thoroughly. Always ensure mattress is completely dry before use.*

OIL PAINTINGS

General stains: If valuable, consult professionals. On others, use picture cleaner. Follow instructions carefully.
● *Never attempt to clean valuable paintings.*
● *Always dust lightly and frequently.*

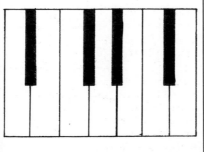

PIANO KEYS

General stains: *Ivory:* If valuable, consult professionals. Otherwise use solution of equal parts turpentine substitute and warm water. *Or* rub with toothpaste. Buff. Dry. *Plastic:* Use warm water plus a few drops of vinegar. Wipe dry.
● *Never let water get between keys. Never attempt to clean valuable pianos.*

PILLOWS

Act fast. Treat covers according to stain. See Fabrics (pp. 21-25). If the filling becomes stained: *Down and feather:* Have professionally washed. *Foam:* Wash in warm soapy water. Rinse. Dry thoroughly. *Synthetic fiber:* Machine or hand-wash. Follow instructions.
● *Never dry-clean synthetic fiber pillows. Never use lighter fluid or strong chlorine solution on fabrics encasing foam rubber.*
● *Always use a cover on your pillow and remove and clean it first without touching pillow. Always ensure pillow is completely dry before use.*

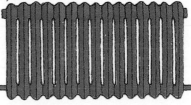

RADIATORS

See Painted Wood (p. 13). Metals (p. 8)
● *Always cover the floor below the radiator when cleaning.*

TELEPHONE

General stains: Rub with turpentine substitute.

Fabrics chart

Fabric	Machine Wash	Hand Wash	Agitation	Rinse	Spinning
White cotton and linen without special finishes.	Very hot to Boil	Hot or boil	Maximum	Normal	Normal
Cotton, linen, modal or rayon articles without special finishes colorfast at hot. Also Denim.	Hot	Hand hot	Maximum	Normal	Normal
White nylon, white polyester/cotton mixtures.	Hot	Hand hot	Medium	Cold	Short spin or drip-dry
Colored nylon, cotton, polyester, rayon with special finishes: acrylic or modacrylic and cotton mixtures: colored cotton and polyester mixtures.	Hand hot	Hand hot.	Medium	Cold	Short spin or drip-dry
Cotton, linen or rayon articles where colorfast at warm but not at hot. Also Elastane.	Warm	Warm	Medium	Normal	Normal
Acrylics, modacrylics; acetate and triacetate, including mixtures with wool; polyester/wool blends.	Warm	Warm	Minimum	Cold	Short spin Do not hand-wring
Wool, including blankets and wool mixtures with cotton or rayon; silk.	Warm.	Warm	Minimum Do not rub	Normal	Normal Do not hand-wring
Silk and printed acetate fabrics not colorfast at warm temperatures.	Cool	Cool	Minimum	Cold	Short spin Do not hand-wring
Cotton articles with special finishes capable of being boiled but requiring drip-drying.	Very hot to Boil	Hand hot or Boil	Maximum	Cold	Drip-dry

	Fabric	Never/Always
Never Wash	Brocade, Silk/Satin/Velvet Felt Fur Leather/Suede Velour Velvet/Velveteen	**Always** have professionally dry-cleaned. **Always** have professionally dry-cleaned. *Or* use an absorbent powder. **Always** have professionally dry-cleaned. See Leather (pp.16-17). **Always** have professionally dry-cleaned. **Always** follow manufacturer's care instructions.
Never Dry Clean	**Polypropylene:** Cournova, Meraklon.	May be machine-washed in warm water. Do not iron. Follow manufacturer's care instructions.

washing guide to everday fabrics.

Brand Names	Never/Always	Special Instructions
	Always wash whites and coloreds separately. Bleaches may be used. Always treat stains before washing. Never use strong acids.	**Linen:** Never use chlorine bleach.
Denim. Modal: Avril, Vincel, Zantrel, Zaryl. **Rayon:** Avril, Delustra, Evlan, Sarille, Viloft, Vincel, Zantrel, Zaryl.	Always wash whites and coloreds separately. Bleaches may be used, test first. Always treat stains before washing. Never use acids or strong alkaline solutions.	**Denim:** Always wash seperately. Never use bleaches. **Linen:** See above. **Modal/Rayon:** Never boil.
Nylon: Antron, Bri-nylon, Cantrece, Celon, Celon Anti-Stat, Counter-Stat, Cumuloft, Enka-comfort, Enkacrepe, Enkalon, Enkasheer, Enka-stat, Miralon, Pavanne, Qiana.	Always wash whites and coloreds separately. Always treat stains before washing.	**Nylon:** Always hand-wash delicate items in cold water. Never use hydrogen peroxide bleach, may use other bleaches.
Polyster: Dacron, Diolen, Fortrel, Lirelle, Ter-lenka, Terylene, Trevira. **Acrylic/Modacrylic:** See below. **Nylon:** See above. **Rayon:** See above.	Always wash whites and colored cottons separately. Always follow manufacturer's care label instructions. Always treat stains before washing. Only use bleach on colorfast fabrics. Test first.	**Nylon:** See above. **Rayon:** Never use shellac solvent/turpentine, acetone, paint brush cleaner or chlorine bleach. Never boil or soak for long. **Acrylic/Modacrylic:** See below.
Elastane: Lycra, Spanzelle, **Rayon:** See above.	Wash white and colored cottons and linens seperately. Always treat stains before washing. Always test before using bleaches. Never use bleaches on non-colorfast fabrics. Test first.	**Rayon:** See above. **Elastene:** Never use chlorine bleach. Never dry in the sun or artificially.
Acetate: Celesta, Dicel. **Acrylics:** Acrilan, Cour-telle, Dralon, Orlon. **Modacrylic:** Acrilan SEF, Kanekalon, Teklan. **Triacetate:** Arnel, Rhonel, Tricel, Tricelon. **Polyester:** See above.	Always follow manufacturer's care instructions. Always treat stains before washing. Always test first before using bleaches.	**Acetate / Acrylic / Modacrylic / Triacetate:** Never use acetone, paint brush cleaner, shellac solvent/turpentine, white vinegar. Always handle acetone gently. Never use bleaches on mod-acrylics. **Wool:** See below.
Wool: Angora, Cashmere. **Rayon:** See above.	Always follow manufacturer's care instructions. Always treat stains before washing. Always test first before using bleaches.	**Rayon:** See above. **Silk:** Never use soap, alka-lies, ammonia, chlorine bleach or enzyme deter-gent. Never rub silk, squeeze only. Never dry in the sun or artificially. **Wool:** Never use hydrogen peroxide plus ammonia, or ammonia alone, or alkalies or water-softeners on wool or wool mixtures. Never soak in chlorine bleach or enzyme detergent for long. Always use Woolite and cold water if washing by hand.
Acetate: See above.	Always follow manufacturer's care instructions. Always treat stains before washing. Test first before using bleaches.	**Acetate:** See above. **Silk:** See above.
	Always follow manufacturer's care instructions. Always treat stains before washing. Always test first before using bleaches. Always wash whites and coloreds separately.	

Fabrics chart

	Fabric	Never/Always
Never Machine Wash	Canvas	Wipe with a damp cloth or scrub with soap lather. Never over-wet.
	Wool, Cashmere, Angora	**Always** follow manufacturer's care instructions. May be machine-washed, but it is advisable not to do so.
	Fur Fabric	**Always** follow manufacturer's care instructions. May be dry-cleaned professionally.
	Lace	**Antique:** Soak in cold distilled water, or consult professionals. **Machine-made:** See Nylon/Polyester.
	Metallic Fibers (Lurex)	Follow manufacturer's care instructions.
	PVC	Wipe clean with a damp cloth. Treat stains at once.
Never Use Chlorine Bleach		**Never** use on linen, non-colorfast fabrics, rayon, elastane, modacrylic, wool, silk. **Never** use on crease-resistant, drip-dry, embossed or pique fabrics. Always test first.

CLEANING METHODS

The following cleaning methods are general techniques for cleaning fabrics and carpets. Refer to this section when Cleaning Method is called for in the text.

METHOD 1: DRY-CLEANING

Stain removal: 1. Remove surface deposit. 2. If possible, put clean white cotton wool or similar absorbent pad under fabric with wrong side of fabric facing upwards. 3. Dab, *not rub*, carefully with another clean pad saturated with the recommended dry-cleaning solvent (or see Dry-Cleaner Solutions (p. 2) under Cleaning Agents). 4. Blot dry after each application. 5. Launder or dry-clean as usual.

- *Never pour cleaning agents directly onto surface.*
- *Never over-wet fabric with cleaning agent or rub too hard.*
- *Never let cleaning agents touch rubber-latexed or foam-backed carpets.*
- *Always consult Fabrics Chart (pp. 18-19) and follow manufacturer's instructions if available.*
- *Always consult Cleaning Agents (pp. 2-3) and follow label instructions carefully.*
- *Always test cleaning agent on hidden part of fabric before using. Wait 15 minutes. If fabric is damaged, seek professional advice.*
- *Always use repeated weak applications of cleaning agent, not one strong one.*
- *Always work from the outside towards the middle of the stain to avoid making rings.*
- *Always change pads frequently.*
- *Always seek professional advice if the stain persists.*

METHOD 2: ABSORBENT

Stain removal: 1. Remove surface deposit. 2. Spread the fabric as flat as possible. 3. Apply absorbent powder thickly over stain and flatten gently. 4. Remove when saturated and re-apply as necessary. Or leave 1 hour and remove.

- *Never use absorbent powders on carpets.*
- *Always consult Cleaning Agents (pp.2-3) and follow label instructions carefully.*
- *Always seek professional advice if stain persists.*

METHOD 3: SPONGING AND SOAKING FABRICS

Stain removal: Non-washable fabrics: 1. Remove surface deposit. 2. Use cold water and sponge gently. 3. When possible, stretch stained part of fabric over a bowl and pour cold water through it. Pour from a height of 2-3 feet.

- *Always consult Fabrics Chart (pp. 18-19) and follow manufacturer's care instructions if available.*
- *Always consult Cleaning Agents (pp. 2-3) and follow label instructions carefully.*
- *Always test cleaning agent on hidden part of fabric before using.*

Stain removal: Washable fabrics: Act fast. 1. Remove surface deposit. 2. Rinse with cold or warm water. 3. Soak in solution of cleaning agent recommended. If stain persists, put clean white cotton wool or similar absorbent pad under fabric with fabric wrong side up. 4. Sponge with cleaning solution on another clean pad. 5. Rinse with clear water. Blot dry. 6. Repeat if necessary.

- *Never soak wool, silk, non-colorfast or flame-proof fabrics.*
- *Always consult Fabrics Chart (pp. 18-19) and follow manufacturer's care instructions if available.*
- *Always consult Cleaning Agents (pp. 2-3) and follow label instructions carefully.*
- *Always test cleaning agent on hidden part of fabric before using:* 1. *Apply cleaning agent to fabric.* 2. *Place wet fabric between two white cloths.* 3. *Apply warm iron. If cloths remain unmarked, fabric is colorfast. If non-colorfast, seek professional advice.*

METHOD 4: SPONGING AND SOAKING UPHOLSTERY AND CARPETS

Stain removal: 1. Use foam shampoo or dissolve upholstery or liquid carpet shampoo in warm water until it foams. 2. Sponge stain lightly with foam. Blot often. 3. Rinse with cold water by sponging gently. 4. If stain persists leave to dry then use Dry-Cleaning Method 1. Or seek professional advice. Or, for small stains, use a spotting kit or spot remover. Follow instructions.

- *Never over-wet fabric or carpet.*
- *Never use household detergent on upholstery.*
- *Never use soap, soap powder or soda on carpets.*
- *Always consult Fabrics Chart (pp. 18-19) and follow manufacturer's care instructions if available.*
- *Always consult Cleaning Agents (pp. 2-3) and follow label instructions carefully.*
- *Always test cleaning agent on hidden part of fabric/carpet before using. If fabric/carpet is damaged seek professional advice.*
- *Use lather only if using detergent on carpets. Dry carpet outside if possible or else lift clear of floor to dry.*

METHOD 5: BOILING WATER (FOR WHITE AND COLORFAST LINENS ONLY).

Stain removal: 1. Stretch fabric over basin. 2. Sprinkle stain with a little detergent or dry borax. 3. Pour boiling water through stained part of fabric from height of 2-3 feet. Rinse. 4. If stain persists, see Method 1, Method 3 or Method 4.

METHOD 6: BLEACHING

- *Never use on carpets or upholstery.*
- *Always consult Fabrics Chart (pp. 18-19) and follow manufacturer's care instructions if available.*
- *Always consult Cleaning Agents (pp. 2-3) and follow label instructions carefully.*
- *Always test cleaning agents on hidden part of fabric before using.*

First aid (fabrics, including upholstery)

FIRST AID

1. Act fast. The faster you act the milder the remedy needed.

2. Blot dry or remove surface deposit.

3. **Grease stains:** Cover with an absorbent powder. **Fruit, wine or beetroot stains:** Cover with salt. **Other stains:** Rinse with cold water.

4. Always follow manufacturer's care instructions if available.

5. Find relevant stain in FABRICS (pp. 21-25) or UPHOLSTERY (pp. 26-27) sections. Read relevant section of Cleaning Methods (p. 20) and follow instructions carefully.

6. If necessary, test cleaning agent first in an inconspicuous place.

7. Be cautious. If in doubt or unable to identify stain, consult professionals.

8. Once stain is treated, dry treated fabric quickly and evenly with hair-dryer or fan heater to prevent discoloration, unless otherwise noted.

9. After treating stain, launder or dry-clean as usual for best results.

10. If the stain persists, consult professionals.

Cleaning Methods referred to in text will be found on page 20. Always refer to before taking action.

Animal stains: See Urine or Vomit (column 3).

Bird droppings: 1. Soak. 2. If necessary, use hydrogen peroxide or bleach solution, *but not on nylon. Or* use dry-cleaner solution (Method 1).

Blood: *Washable fabrics:* 1. Soak immediately in cold water (Method 3). 2. Wash in warm enzyme detergent solution or upholstery shampoo (Method 3). *Or* soak in hydrogen peroxide solution. For dried stains use ammonia (Method 3). Then wash as above. *Non-washable fabrics:* 1. Wipe or brush off surplus. 2. Sponge with cold water plus few drops ammonia (Method 3). Rinse. Blot well. *Or* use sponge with hydrogen peroxide plus ammonia (Method 3). Leave 10 minutes. Rinse.

Cologne: See Perfume.

Cosmetics: See Foundation Cream, Lipstick.

Deodorant: 1. Soak in white vinegar or ammonia solution (Method 3). 2. If necessary, use turpentine substitute (Method 1).

Droppings: See Vomit.

Foundation Cream: *Washable fabrics:* 1. Remove deposit. 2. Soak in ammonia solution (Method 3). Rinse. 3. Launder as usual. *Dried stains:* 1. Brush off excess. 2. Loosen with glycerine solution. Rinse. 3. Launder as usual. *Non-washable fabrics:* 1. Remove deposit. 2. Use dry-cleaner solution (Method 1). *Or* use absorbent powder (Method 2). *Or* use upholstery spotting kit.

Hair oil/cream: See Grease (p. 24).

Hair spray: Either sponge with cold water, or use turpentine substitute, acetone or amyl acetate (Method 1).

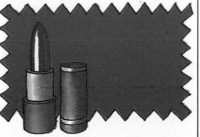

Lipstick: 1. Sponge with eucalyptus oil or glycerine. Rinse. 2. Use lighter fluid or dry-cleaner solution (Method 1).

Indelible lipstick: 1. Rub with lard. 2. Use dry-cleaner solution (Method 1).

Mascara: Use dry-cleaner solution (Method

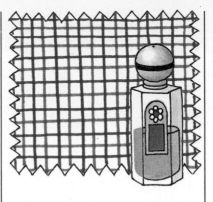

1). *Or* sponge with ammonia solution (Method 3). Rinse.

Perfume: 1. Sponge with water at once. 2. Use glycerine solution. Rinse. 3. Launder if possible. Have delicate fabrics dry-cleaned professionally.

Perspiration: 1. Sponge with warm enzyme detergent solution (Method 3). *Or* use ammonia solution. *Old stains:* 1. Use white vinegar solution (Method 3). 2. If necessary, use hydrogen peroxide or chlorine bleach solution (Method 6). *Or* dry-cleaner solution (Method 1).

Sun-tan oil: Soak or sponge with enzyme detergent solution (Method 3).

Sweat: See Perspiration (above).

Urine: *Washable fabrics:* 1. Rinse in cold water. 2. Launder as normal. *Dried stains:* Soak in enzyme detergent solution (Method 3). 2. Use hydrogen peroxide plus ammonia solution if necessary (Method 6). *Non-washable fabrics:* 1. Sponge with cold water. 2. Sponge with white vinegar solution (Method 3). Have dried stains dry-cleaned professionally.

Vomit: *Washable fabrics:* 1. Remove deposit. 2. Rinse with cold running water. 3. Soak in enzyme detergent solution (Method 3). 4. Launder as normal. *Non-washable fabrics:* 1. Remove deposit. 2. Sponge with ammonia solution (Method 3). *Or* use upholstery spotting kit. 3. If necessary, have dry-cleaned professionally.

Cleaning Methods referred to in
text will be found on page 20.
Always refer to before taking action.

Alcohol: 1. Wipe up immediately. 2. Sponge with warm water. 3. Wash or sponge with liquid detergent solution (Method 3). Rinse with warm water, or use an upholstery spotting kit. 4. If necessary, use chlorine bleach or hydrogen peroxide solution (Method 6).

Baked beans: 1. Soak in enzyme detergent (Method 3). 2. Use dry-cleaner solution (Method 1).

Beer: *Washable fabrics:* For dried stains on white cottons or linens use hydrogen peroxide solution. For dried stains on colored fabrics sponge with white vinegar (Method 3). *Non-washable fabrics:* Use detergent or carpet shampoo (Method 3). For dried stains sponge with white vinegar solution (Method 3). *Or* use dry-cleaner solution. *Or* an upholstery spotting kit.

Beetroot: Soak in enzyme detergent solution (Method 3).
Bottled Sauces: See Ketchup (p. 23).
Brandy: See Alcohol (above).

Butter: See Grease (p. 24).
Chewing gum: 1. Chill with ice cube to harden. 2. Scrape off. 3. Use dry-cleaner solution (Method 1). 4. Wash or sponge with warm water.

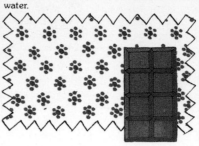

Chocolate/Cocoa: 1. Scrape off deposit. 2. Use enzyme detergent or borax solution (Method 3). Or use boiling water from height (Method 5). 3. If stain persists, and for non-washable fabrics, use dry-cleaner solution (Method 1).
Chutney: See Jam (p. 23).
Cod-liver oil: *Washable fabrics:* Wash immediately in detergent solution. *Dried stains:* 1. Use dry-cleaner solution (Method 1). 2. If marks remain, lubricate with glycerine solution. Rinse. 3. Launder as usual. 4. If necessary, use hydrogen peroxide solution. *Non-washable fabrics:* Use dry-cleaner solution (Method 1). *Woolens:* Sponge immediately with mild detergent solution. Wash. On dried stains use liquid stain remover (Method 1). Wash. Impossible to remove old stains.

Coffee: 1. Sponge with borax solution (Method 3). Loosen dried stains with glycerine solution. 2. Use chlorine bleach if necessary. Or, on certain fabrics, pour boiling water from height (Method 5), using borax if necessary.

Cream: *Washable fabrics:* 1. Use enzyme detergent or borax (Method 3). 2. When dry, use dry-cleaner solution (Method 1). *Non-washable fabrics:* 1. Use dry-cleaner solution (Method 1). 2. Sponge carefully with cold water.

Curry: *Washable fabrics:* 1. Remove deposits. 2. Soften with glycerine solution. 3. Use enzyme detergent or ammonia solution (Method 3). 4. Bleach if necessary. *Non-washable fabrics:* 1. Remove deposit. 2. Use ammonia or borax solution (Method 1). 3. If necessary, have professionally dry-cleaned.

Egg: *Washable fabrics:* 1. Scrape off deposit. 2. Sponge or soak with cold salt water. 3. Use enzyme detergent solution (Method 3). 4. Use an aerosol dry-cleaner to remove any traces. *Non-washable fabrics:* 1. Remove deposit. 2. Sponge with cold salt water. 3. When dry, use dry-cleaner solution (Method 1).
Fats: See Grease (p. 24).
Fish slime: 1. Soak or sponge with salt water. Rinse. 2. Wash as usual.

Fruit/fruit juice: *Washable fabrics:* 1. Sponge or soak immediately in cold salt water or milk. 2. If necessary, sponge with white vinegar or use hydrogen peroxide (Method 6). *Dried stains:* 1. Loosen with glycerine solution. 2. Soak in enzyme detergent solution (Method 3). *Non-washable fabrics:* 1. Sponge with cold water. 2. When dry, use dry-cleaner solution (Method 1) or use upholstery spotting kit. *White and colorfast linens:* 1. Cover stain with salt. 2. Use boiling water (Method 5) plus borax. *Or* use color and stain remover.

Gravy: *Washable fabrics:* 1. Remove deposit. 2. Sponge or soak with cold water. 3. Use dry-cleaner solution (Method 1). *Dried stains:* 1. Soak in enzyme detergent solution (Method 3). 2. Wash. *Non-washable fabrics:* 1. Remove deposit. 2. Sponge with cold water. *Or* apply absorbent powder (Method 2). *Or* use dry-cleaner solution (Method 1).

Honey: Soak or sponge with enzyme detergent solution (Method 3). *Or* use dry-cleaner solution (Method 1).

Ice cream: See Cream (p. 22).

Jam/marmalade: 1. Remove deposit. 2. Sponge or soak with liquid detergent, enzyme detergent or borax solution (Method 3). 3. If necessary, use chlorine bleach (Method 6) *or* dry-cleaner solution (Method 1).

Juice: See Fruit (above).

Ketchup/bottled sauces: *Washable fabrics:* 1. Remove deposit. 2. Sponge with cold liquid detergent solution. Rinse. 3. Soak in enzyme detergent solution (Method 3). *Non-washable fabrics:* 1. Remove deposit. 2. Wipe with cold water. 3. Use dry-cleaner solution (Method 1) when dry. 4. If necessary, have dry-cleaned professionally.

Liqueurs: See Alcohol (p. 22).

Margarine: See Cream (p. 22).

Marmalade: See Jam (column 1).

Mayonnaise: See Cream (p. 22).

Milk: 1. Sponge or soak in cold water. 2. Launder as usual. 3. If necessary, use upholstery spotting kit *or* dry-cleaner solution (Method 1).

Mustard: 1. Sponge or soak in mild detergent solution. 2. Use ammonia solution on remaining stain (Method 3). 3. Launder if possible. *Or* sponge with hydrogen peroxide (Method 1) on suitable fabrics. On fabrics that ring-mark easily, dry-clean professionally.

Salad dressing: See Grease (above).

Sauces: See Cream (p. 22).

Soft drinks: See Fruit Juice (column 1).

Soup: See Ketchup (above).

Syrup: See Jam (column 1).

Tea: See Coffee. *Or* use an absorbent powder (Method 2).

Tomato juice: See Fruit (column 1).

Treacle: See Jam (column 1).

Turmeric: See Curry (p. 22).

Vinegar: 1. Soak or sponge in enzyme detergent solution (Method 3). 2. Launder if possible. 3. If the color of the fabric has been affected, see Acids (p. 24).

Wine: *Washable fabrics:* 1. Squirt with soda water. *Or* saturate red wine stain with white wine. *Or* cover with salt, rub off when dry. 2. Use boiling water from height (Method 5). *Or* soak in borax or enzyme detergent solution (Method 3). 3. If necessary, use dry-cleaner solution (Method 1) or hydrogen peroxide (Method 6). *Non-washable fabrics:* Act fast. 1. Sponge with warm water. *Or* blot stain and cover with absorbent powder (Method 2). Repeat as necessary. 2. Use glycerine solution on dried stains. 3. Sponge with warm detergent solution (Method 3), rinse. *Or* use an upholstery spotting kit.

Yogurt: 1. Remove deposit. 2. Use dry-cleaner solution (Method 1).

Zabaglione: 1. Remove deposit. 2. Use dry-cleaner solution (Method 1). *Or* soak in enzyme detergent solution (Method 3) where possible.

Food and drink stains

23

Cleaning Methods referred to in text will be found on page 20. Always refer to before taking action.

Acids (sulphuric, hydrochloric, acetic or vinegar): 1. Use cold water (Method 3). 2. Sponge with ammonia or baking soda solution (1 teaspoon to 1 cup water). Rinse. Note: Strong acids may cause permanent damage.

Adhesives: Some now have their own special solvents which may be obtained from the manufacturer. Follow instructions.

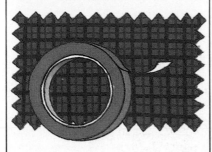

Adhesive tape: Use dry-cleaner solution (Method 1).

Clear and contact adhesives: 1. Use non-oily nail polish remover, acetone or amyl acetate (Method 1). 2. If necessary use bleach (Method 6).

Epoxy resin: Use acetone, amyl acetate or cellulose thinners. On synthetic fibers use lighter fluid (Method 1). When dry, stains cannot be removed.

Latex adhesive: *If wet:* remove with a damp cloth. *If dry:* 1. Scrape off surplus. 2. Use dry-cleaner solution or paint-brush remover (Method 1). *Or* use manufacturer's solvent.

Model-making glue: 1. Wipe off surplus. 2. Use dry-cleaner solution or amyl acetate (Method 1). When dry, stains cannot be removed.

Alkalies (ammonia/washing soda): 1. Sponge immediately with cold water. 2. Use lemon juice, white vinegar or developer solution (Method 1). Note: Strong alkalies may cause permanent damage.

Ballpoint: See Ink (column 3).

Battery acids: See Acids (column 1).

Burns: See Scorch Marks (p. 25).

Candle wax: 1. Scrape off deposit. 2. Place blotting paper over, and if possible, under fabric and press quickly with a warm iron. Repeat until wax is absorbed. Change paper often. 3. Remove color traces with turpentine substitute or dry-cleaner solution (Method 1). 4. If necessary, use chlorine bleach (Method 6). Rinse. *Or* pour boiling water from height through strong fabrics (Method 5).

Carbon paper: Use turpentine substitute or dry-cleaner solution (Method 1).

Crayon: Use dry-cleaner solution or lighter fluid (Method 1).

Creosote: Use eucalyptus oil, lighter fluid or dry cleaner solution (Method 1).

Dyes: *Washable fabrics:* 1. Soak in enzyme detergent solution (Method 3). 2. If necessary use chlorine bleach or hydrogen peroxide (Method 6). *Or* use color and stain remover. *Non-washable fabrics:* Use turpentine substitute plus a few drops of ammonia (Method 1).

Felt-tip: See Ink (column 3).

Flower stains: See Grass (below).

Glue: See Adhesives (column 1).

Grass: 1. Use eucalyptus oil, glycerine or turpentine substitute (Method 1). Rinse. *Or* use equal parts of cream of tartar and salt (Method 2). Remove after 10 minutes. 2. If necessary, use dry-cleaner solution (Method 1), chlorine bleach or hydrogen peroxide (Method 6).

Grease: *Washable fabrics:* 1. Remove deposit. 2. Use absorbent powder (Method 2). *Or* use blotting paper and warm iron (See Candle Wax) (column 2). 3. Wash in warm soapflake solution (Method 3). 4. If necessary, use dry-cleaner solution (Method 1). *Non-washable fabrics:* 1. Scrape off deposit. 2. Use absorbent or warm iron method (see above). 3. Use dry-cleaner solution (Method 1) if necessary. *Heavy stains:* Use paint brush cleaner (Method 1).

Ink, ballpoint or felt-tip: 1. Use turpentine substitute (Method 1) or use glycerine with ammonia solution (Method 1). Keep MOIST. Blot often. 2. If necessary, use chlorine bleach solution (Method 6) or dry-cleaner solution (Method 1). *Polyester:* Spray ballpoint stain with hair spray. Rub off with clean cloth.

Ink, Indian: Act fast. 1. Soak or sponge with cold water. 2. Wash with liquid detergent or soapflake solution. 3. Soak or sponge in ammonia solution (Method 3). Rinse. 4. If color is affected, sponge with white vinegar. 5. If necessary, consult professionals.

Ink, printing: Sponge with turpentine (Method 1).

Ink, writing: *Washable fabrics:* 1. Sponge or soak with cold water or milk. 2. Use enzyme detergent solution (Method 3). 3. If necessary, use dry-cleaner solution (Method 1). *Or* use chlorine bleach or hydrogen peroxide solution (Method 6). 4. If yellow stains remain, see Rust (p. 25). *Non-washable fabrics:* 1. Use absorbent powder (Method 2). 2. Sponge with enzyme detergent solution or dry-cleaner solution. See Washable (above).

Iodine: *Washable fabrics:* 1. Sponge or soak immediately in water. 2. Sponge in detergent solution (Method 3) or have dry-cleaned professionally. *Non-washable fabrics:* Use alcohol (Method 1) or have dry-cleaned professionally.

Iron rust: See Rust (p. 25).

Lead pencil: 1. Use an eraser. 2. Use dry-cleaner solution or turpentine substitute (Method 1) if necessary.

Medicine, iron-based: See Rust (column 2).

Medicine, syrup-based: Wash or sponge with soapy solution (Method 3).

Medicine, tar-based: 1. Rub with vaseline or lard. 2. Use dry-cleaner solution (Method 1). 3. If any color remains, use turpentine substitute (Method 1) or have professionally dry-cleaned.

Metal polish: 1. Remove deposit. 2. Use turpentine substitute or lighter fluid (Method 1). 3. Use dry-cleaner solution (Method 1).

Mildew: *Washable fabrics:* 1. Moisten with lemon or lime juice and salt. Dry in the sun. *Or* use hard soap or enzyme detergent solution (Method 3). Dry in the sun. 2. If necessary, use hydrogen peroxide or chlorine bleach solution (Method 6). *Non-washable fabrics:* Have dry-cleaned professionally.

Mud: 1. Remove deposit. 2. Sponge or soak in cold water or mild detergent solution (Method 3). Rinse. *Dried stains:* 1. Brush. 2. Use dry-cleaner solution (Method 1) if necessary.

Nail polish: 1. Remove deposit. 2. Use amyl acetate or non-oily nail polish remover (Method 1). 3. Use turpentine substitute (Method 1) if necessary.

Nicotine: Use eucalyptus oil or turpentine substitute (Method 1). *Or* soak in enzyme detergent solution (Method 3). Or use hydrogen peroxide (Method 6).

Oil: 1. Use absorbent powder (Method 2). 2. Use dry-cleaner solution (Method 1) if necessary *or* cover with a paste of sugar and water before laundering.

Paint, oil-based: 1. Remove deposit. 2. Sponge with turpentine substitute or paint brush cleaner (Method 1). Test first. 3. Sponge with cold water. 4. Launder if possible.

Paint, water-based: 1. Remove deposit. 2. Sponge with cold water. 3. Launder if possible. *Dried paint:* Use turpentine substitute or paint brush cleaner (Method 1).

Paraffin: See Candle Wax (p. 24).

Pencil: See Lead Pencil (p. 24).

Plasticine: 1. Remove deposit. 2. Use dry-cleaner solution or lighter fluid (Method 1) on small areas. Test first. 3. Launder if possible.

Resins: See Creosote (p. 24).

Rust: *Washable fabrics:* Rub with lemon or lime juice and salt. Dry in the sun. *Or* rub with lemon or lime juice and hold in the steam from a kettle for 2 minutes. *Or* boil in solution of 1 pint water, 4 tablespoons cream of tartar (Method 3). Rinse. *Or* use rust remover. *Non-washable fabrics:* Have cleaned professionally

Sand: 1. Brush off excess. 2. Soak or sponge in enzyme detergent solution (Method 3). 3. Use hydrogen peroxide *or* chlorine bleach (Method 6).

Scorch marks: *Washable fabrics:* Soak in borax, hydrogen peroxide or ammonia solution (Method 3). Rinse. Note: May be impossible to remove from silk or wool or if the cloth fibers have been burned. *Non-washable fabrics:* 1. Rub with glycerine solution. Rinse. 2. If necessary, sponge with borax solution (Method 3).

Shellac: Act fast. 1. Use dry-cleaner solution or turpentine substitute (Method 1). 2. Launder if possible.

Shoe polish: *Washable fabrics:* 1. Remove deposit. 2. Use dry-cleaner solution or turpentine substitute (Method 1). 3. Soak in ammonia solution (Method 3). 4. Launder as usual. *Non-washable fabrics:* 1. Remove deposit. 2. Use turpentine, turpentine substitute or dry-cleaner solution (Method 1). 3. Repeat if necessary. If turpentine or turpentine substitute is used, sponge with warm detergent solution afterwards.

Smoke and soot: *Washable fabrics:* 1. Vacuum deposit. 2. Soak in enzyme detergent solution (Method 3). 3. Launder as usual. *Non-washable fabrics:* 1. Vacuum deposit. 2. Use an absorbent powder (Method 2). 3. Vacuum again. 4. Use dry-cleaner solution (Method 1). If the stain is large, have dry-cleaned professionally.

Soap: Re-wash article and rinse thoroughly.

Tar: *Washable fabrics:* 1. Remove deposit. 2. Use eucalyptus oil (Method 1). 3. Launder as usual. *Non-washable fabrics:* 1. Remove deposit. 2. Use glycerine solution. Rinse. 3. If necessary, use dry-cleaner solution, turpentine or lighter fluid (Method 1).

Tobacco: See Grass (p. 24).

Transfer patterns: Use turpentine substitute (Method 1).

Unidentified stains: Have professionally dry-cleaned.

Varnish: See Shellac (column 2). If cellulose or polyurethane, see Paint (column 2).

Water spots: Hold items in the steam from a boiling kettle or have dry-cleaned professionally.

Wax: See Candle Wax (p. 24).

General
stains

BEDSPREADS: See Fabrics (pp. 21-25).

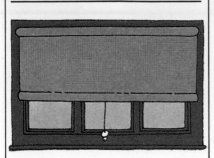

BLINDS, CANVAS ROLLER OR ROMAN

Light spots: Use soft eraser.
Rips/Tears: Mend with clear nail polish.
General stains: *Washable fabrics:* 1. Scrub with warm soapy water. 2. Rinse with cold water. Air dry. *Non-washable fabrics:* Rub with flour or cornmeal on rough flannel cloth.

BLINDS, VENETIAN

General Stains: *Painted/plastic:* Wash one slat at a time with mild soapy water, paintwork cleaner, or turpentine substitute on a soft cloth. *Natural wood:* Clean one slat at a time with liquid furniture polish. Change cloth frequently.
● *Always rinse and dry painted and plastic blinds carefully.*

CURTAINS

● *Never machine wash. Never rub, twist or mangle glass fiber curtains. Never iron glass fiber curtains. Never iron plastic curtains. Never soak rayon curtains.*
● *Always follow manufacturer's care instructions. Always test first. Always remove hooks, curtain weights etc. from curtains before washing. Always wear rubber gloves when washing glass fiber curtains. Always hand-wash delicate fabrics.*
See also Fabrics (pp. 21-25).

UPHOLSTERY, FABRIC/TEXTILE

● *Never over-wet. Never use household detergent. Never use turpentine substitute on acetate, triacetate, modacrylic or rayon upholstery.*
● *Always use a clean cloth. Always test first. Always follow manufacturer's care instructions. Always check on properties of fabric before starting cleaning.*

Adhesives: See Adhesives (p. 24).

Alcohol: See Alcohol (p. 22).

Animal stains: See Urine or Vomit (p. 27).

Ballpoint: See Ink (column 3).

Beer: See Beer (p. 22).

Blood: Rub lightly with paste of cornstarch and cold water. Leave to dry. Brush off. Repeat.

Burns: See Scorch Marks (p. 25).

Butter: See Grease (column 3).

Candle wax: 1. Remove deposit. 2. Cover with blotting paper. Press with warm iron. Repeat until absorbed. Change paper often. 3. Remove color traces with turpentine substitute or dry-cleaner solution (Method 1).

Chewing Gum: See Chewing Gum (p. 22).

Chocolate: 1. Remove deposit. 2. Use dry-cleaner solution (Method 1).

Chutney, Cocoa, Coffee, Crayon, Cream, Curry, Dyes, Egg, Fruit, Fruit Juices, Gin, Glue, Grass, Gravy: See stain under Fabric Section (pp. 21-25).

Grease: Use salt or cornflour (Method 2). Brush off once grease is absorbed.

Hair Oil Cream: Use dry-cleaner solution (Method 1).

Honey: See Honey (p. 30).

Ice Cream: See Cream (p. 22).

Ink, ballpoint: Use turpentine substitute (Method 1) or consult professionals.

Ink, felt-tip: See Ballpoint (above). *Or* use dry-cleaner solution (Method 1).

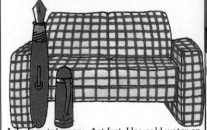

Ink, fountain pen: Act fast. Use cold water or lemon juice (Method 1). Blot. *Or* use upholstery spotting kit.

Jam, Ketchup, Lead Pencil, Lipstick, Mayonnaise, Metal Polish, Mildew, Milk, Mud, Nail Polish: See stain under Fabric Section (pp. 21-25).

Oil: See Grease (above).

Paint, Plasticine, Rust: See stain under Fabric Section (pp. 21-25).

Salad dressing: See Grease (this section).

Upholstery/ Curtains

Sauces: See Cream (p. 22).

Scorch Marks, Shoe Polish, Smoke and Soot, Soft Drinks, Soup, Syrup, Tar, Tea, Tomato Juice: See stain under Fabric Section (pp. 21-25).

Urine/Vomit: 1. Remove deposit. Blot. 2. Use dry-cleaner solution (Method 1). 3. If possible, rinse under cold running water.

Wax: See Candle Wax. (p. 26).

Wine: See Wine (p. 23).

UPHOLSTERY, LEATHER

Ballpoint: Sponge immediately with milk.

Cracking leather: Apply solution of 1 part vinegar to 2 parts linseed oil regularly.

Ink: Sponge immediately with water.

General stains: Use soft cloth moistened with soapflake solution, *or* a damp cloth rubbed over

a bar of glycerine soap.

● *Never use detergent. Never rinse after washing with soap. Never use dry-cleaning fluid, gasoline or ammonia.*

● *Always consult professionals on non-washable leather.*

See also Leather (pp. 16-17).

UPHOLSTERY, TAPESTRY

● *Always have dry-cleaned professionally.*

UPHOLSTERY, VELVET/VELVETEEN

● *Always have dry-cleaned professionally or follow manufacturer's care instructions.*

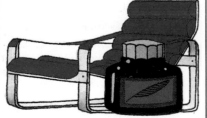

UPHOLSTERY, VINYL AND OTHER PLASTICS

Ballpoint: Consult professionals.

Chewing Gum: 1. Scrape off deposit. 2. Use paraffin or lighter fluid and rub with soft cloth.

Ink: Wipe at once with water or alcohol.

Paint and shoe polish: Wipe immediately. Rub with turpentine.

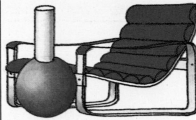

Tar, asphalt and motor oil: Remove immediately with turpentine or lighter fluid.

General stains: Wipe with warm soapy water. Rinse with clean damp cloth. Buff. *Or* use vinyl upholstery cleaner. *Or* use baking soda or vinegar on rough, damp cloth. Wash with warm soapy water.

● *Never over-wet. Never use harsh chemicals, solvents or alcohol-based cleaners. Never use wax polishes.*

● *Always act fast. Always test first.*

See also Vinyl Flooring (p. 11) and Vinyl Wallcoverings (p. 12).

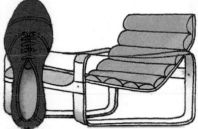

UPHOLSTERY, WATER REPELLANT FABRICS

● *Always have dry-cleaned or follow manufacturer's care instructions.*

> **Cleaning Methods referred to in text will be found on page 20. Always refer to before taking action.**

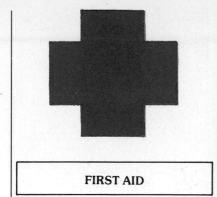

FIRST AID

1. Act fast. The faster you act the milder the remedy needed.
2. Blot liquids or remove surface deposit. Then flood the stain with soda water or cold water. Blot.
3. Always follow manufacturer's care instructions if available.
4. Check carpet fiber and consult Carpets Section (below) for advice on various carpet fibers.
5. Find relevant stain in Carpets Section and read relevant instructions of Cleaning Methods (p. 20) and follow instructions carefully.
6. Test cleaning agent first in an inconspicuous place.
7. Always blot dry before and after using dry-cleaner solutions.
8. Be cautious. If in doubt or unable to identify stain, consult professionals.
9. After treating stain, shampoo whole carpet for best results.
10. If stain persists, consult professionals.

TYPES OF CARPETS AND RUGS

Acetate and triacetate carpets
- *Never use acetone, paint brush cleaner or turpentine substitute.*

Dhurries (Indian cotton rugs)
- *Always remove from floor immediately and have professionally cleaned.*

Felt carpets
- *Always have professionally cleaned.*

Fur/shaggy rugs
- *Always have professionally cleaned.*

Oriental/antique rugs
- *Always have professionally cleaned.*

Rush/sisal matting
Act fast.
Grease: Use aerosol dry-cleaner solution (Method 1). *Non-greasy stains:* Use carpet shampoo (Method 4).
- *Never over-wet. Never use detergents, ammonia, washing soda, strong alkalies or household soap.*
- *Always follow manufacturer's care instructions.*

Skin rugs
- *Always have professionally cleaned*

Woolen carpets
- *Never use ammonia.*

Cleaning Methods referred to in text will be found on page 20. Always refer to before taking action.

Acids: See Acids under Fabric Section (p. 24)

Adhesives: See Adhesives under Fabric Section (p. 24). If stains are indelible, trim carpet with scissors.

Animal Stains: See Urine/Vomit (p. 29).

Ballpoint: See Ink (p. 29).

Battery Acid: Act fast. Blot. Apply weak solution of borax (Method 4). Be careful.

Blood: Act fast. Flush with soda water or cold water (see First Aid). Blot. *Or* use carpet spotting kit (Method 4) for difficult to remove dried stains.

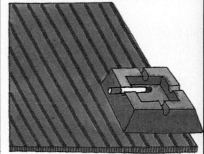

Burns: Trim burned fibers with scissors. Then use carpet shampoo plus 1 teaspoon white vinegar (Method 4). Rinse. Blot. Consult professionals for extensive burns and burns on synthetic fiber carpets.

Candle Wax: 1. Remove deposit. 2. Place blotting paper over carpet (and under if possible). Press with warm iron. Repeat until wax is absorbed. Change paper often. 3. Remove color traces with turpentine substitute (Method 1).

Crayon: Use dry-cleaner solution or lighter fluid (Method 1).

Droppings: See Vomit (column 3).

Dyes: Use turpentine substitute plus a few drops of ammonia (Method 1). Test first.

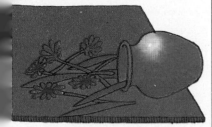

Flower Stains: See Grass (below).

Glue: See Adhesives (p. 24). If stains are indelible, trim carpet with scissors.

Grass: 1. Use turpentine substitute (Method 1). 2. Use carpet shampoo (Method 4).

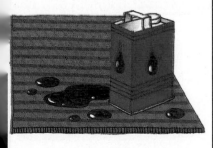

Grease: 1. Remove deposit. 2. Use dry-cleaner solution (Method 1) or use iron and blotting paper. See Candle Wax (p. 28). 3. Use carpet shampoo (Method 4).

Hair oil/cream: See Grease (above).

Ink, ballpoint: Use turpentine substitute plus a little white vinegar (Method 1). Or use vinegar and milk (Method 4). Blot. Then see Fountain Pen Ink (below).

Ink, fountain pen: 1. Flush with soda water. Blot 2. Use a solution of equal parts white vinegar and water (Method 4). Blot. 3. Use carpet shampoo. 4. If necessary, consult professionals or ink manufacturer.

Metal Polish: 1. Remove deposit. 2. Use turpentine substitute (Method 1). 3. Shampoo.

Mud: 1. Vacuum when dry. 2. Use carpet spotting kit or shampoo (Method 4). 3. Use turpentine substitute (Method 1) on remaining color.

Nail polish: 1. Remove deposit. 2. Use amyl acetate or non-oily nail polish remover (Method 1). Test first. 3. Then use carpet shampoo (Method 4).

Oil: See Grease (column 1).

Paint: 1. Remove deposit. 2. Use dry-cleaner solution (Method 1). 3. Use carpet shampoo (Method 4).

Paraffin Oil: See Grease (column 1). Have large areas professionally dry-cleaned.

Plasticine: See Plasticine under Fabrics (p. 25).

Rust: Use rust remover. Follow instructions. Shampoo if necessary (Method 4).

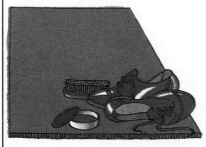

Scorch marks: See Burns (p. 28).

Shoe polish: 1. Remove deposit. 2. Use aerosol dry-cleaner or turpentine substitute (Method 1). Repeat if necessary 3. Shampoo.

Soot: 1. Vacuum carefully. 2. Use aerosol dry-cleaner solution (Method 1). 3. Shampoo (Method 4). Have large areas professionally cleaned.

Tar: 1. Remove deposit. 2. Rub with glycerine solution. Rinse. Blot. 3. Use dry-cleaner solution (Method 1). 4. If necessary, rub with eucalyptus oil or paint brush cleaner (Method 1). 5. Shampoo (Method 4).

Urine: 1. Flush with soda water or sponge with white vinegar solution (Method 4). Blot. 2. Shampoo with added antiseptic (Method 4).

Vomit: 1. Remove deposit. 2. Flush with soda water. Blot. Or sponge with borax solution (Method 4). 3. Shampoo with added antiseptic.

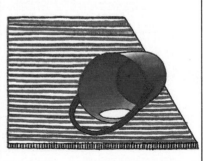

Water: Mop up immediately. Dry outside if possible or raise carpet from the floor. If flooded, call professionals.

Cleaning Methods referred to in text will be found on page 20. Always refer to before taking action.

Alcohol: 1. Blot. 2. Squirt with soda water or sponge with warm water (Method 4). 3. Shampoo. 4. If necessary, rub with glycerine solution. Rinse. *Dried stains:* Use turpentine substitute.

Beer: 1. Flush with soda water or warm water (Method 4). Blot. 2. If necessary, use carpet shampoo or spotting kit (Method 4). 3. Sponge old stains with turpentine substitute (Method 1).

Beetroot: See Fruit (column 2).

Butter: See Grease (p. 29).

Chewing Gum: See Chewing Gum under Fabric Section (p. 22).

Chocolate: 1. Remove deposit. 2. Use carpet shampoo (Method 4). Rinse. Blot dry. 2. If necessary use liquid dry-cleaner (Method 1).

Chutney: See Jam (column 2).

Cocoa: See Chocolate. *Dried stains:* Sponge with borax solution (Method 4). Blot. If necessary, rub with glycerine solution.

Coffee: 1. Blot. 2. Flush with soda water or cold water (Method 4). Blot. 3. If necessary, use carpet shampoo or spotting kit (Method 4). 4. When dry, remove traces with dry-cleaner solution (Method 1).

Cream: Remove deposit. Use dry-cleaner solution (Method 1).

Curry: 1. Remove deposit. 2. Rub with borax solution (Method 4) or glycerine solution. Rinse. Blot. Have large stains professionally cleaned.

Egg: Remove deposit. Use liquid dry-cleaner solution (Method 1) *or* carpet shampoo if necessary (Method 4).

Fats: See Grease (p. 29).

Fruit and Fruit Juices: 1. Remove deposit or blot. 2. Use carpet shampoo (Method 4). 3. If necessary, use turpentine substitute (Method 1) or carpet spotting kit (Method 4).

Gravy: 1. Remove deposit. Blot. 2. Use liquid dry-cleaner solution (Method 1). 3. Use carpet shampoo (Method 4).

Honey: 1. Remove deposit. 2. Use dry-cleaner solution (Method 1). 3. Shampoo if necessary (Method 4).

Ice Cream: 1. Remove deposit. 2. Wipe with damp cloth. 3. Use carpet shampoo (Method 4). 4. If necessary, use dry-cleaner solution (Method 1).

Jam/Marmalade: 1. Remove deposit. 2. Use carpet shampoo (Method 4). 3. If necessary, use turpentine substitute (Method 1).

Juice: See Fruit (above).

Ketchup/Bottled Sauces: 1. Remove deposit. 2. Sponge with warm water or carpet shampoo (Method 4). 3. If necessary use dry-cleaner solution (Method 1). *Dried stains:* Rub with glycerine solution before shampooing.

Margarine: See Grease. (p. 29).

Mayonnaise: See Cream (above).

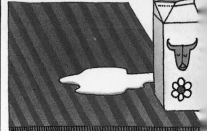

Milk: 1. Flush with soda water or warm water (Method 4). Blot. 2. Use carpet shampoo or spotting kit (Method 4). 3. If necessary use dry-cleaner solution (Method 1).

Salad dressing: See Grease (p. 29).

Salt: Vacuum well.

Sauces: See Cream (column 2).

Soft drinks: See Fruit (column 2).

Soup: See Ketchup (column 2).

Syrup: See Jam (column 2).

Tea: See Coffee. *Dried stains:* Use borax solution (Method 4).

Tomato juice: See Fruit (column 2).

Wine: Act fast. 1. Flush with soda water or warm water. Or use white wine for red wine stains (Method 4). Blot. 2. Shampoo. *Dried stains:* Sponge with turpentine substitute (Method 1). Test first.

● *Never use soap, soap powder or soda on carpets.*

● *Always leave carpet pile leaning in correct direction.*

Food and drink stains

Carpets and rugs 2